Berlitz

Tenerife

Front cover: A traditional windmill

Right: A scarlet macaw at Loro Parque in
Puerto de la Cruz

TOP 10 ATTRACTIONS

La Orotava La Orotava's Casa de los Balcones is the best example of a traditional town mansion *(page 47)*

El Teide • This dramatic, snowcapped volcano is Spain's highest mountain *(page 52)*

Playa de las Teresitas Stretching 1.5km (1 mile), the main beach for Santa Cruz has the most golden sand on the island *(page 33)*

Castillo de San Miguel The castle in Garachico has great views out to sea *(page 62)*

San Cristóbal de la Laguna With many lovely old buildings, the former capital is a UNESCO World Heritage Site *(page 34)*

Jardín Botánico in Puerto de la Cruz The garden was used as a staging post for New World flora and is full of exotic plants *(page 44)*

Museo de la Naturaleza y el Hombre Located in Santa Cruz, this is Tenerife's largest museum *(page 29)*

Los Gigantes Beneath sheer cliffs that give it its name, the resort is a major centre for diving and boat trips *(page 67)*

Masca A beautiful, remote village with views down to the sea *(page 65)*

Parque Etnográfico Pirámides de Güímar These structures are thought to be pyramids built for sun worship *(page 77)*

80

45

94

CONTENTS

76

71

67

INTRODUCTION

Time signals on state radio and television in Spain give two times: one for mainland Spain and one for 'Las Canarias'. Adrift in the Atlantic Ocean more than 1,000km (620 miles) to the south, and 115km (70 miles) from the west coast of Africa, Tenerife and the 12 other islands that make up the Canary archipelago don't see the sun rise until around one hour later than their mainland compatriots.

At just over 2,000 sq km (around 800 sq miles), Tenerife is the largest of these volcanic cones that began to erupt from the depths of the Atlantic bed 20 million years ago. Six are tiny and uninhabited. Of the others, the three closest to Africa (Gran Canaria, Lanzarote and Fuerteventura) are the oldest, formed 10 million years before Tenerife. Finally, some 2 million years after that, the Canary's other western isles of La Palma, La Gomera and El Hierro burst into life.

Volcanic Landscape

On a clear day all the islands can be seen from the top of Tenerife's Pico del Teide, at 3,718m (12,195ft) the highest mountain in the whole of Spain. Its peak was formed a million years ago inside the crater of a former, collapsed volcano, the Circo de Cañadas, where the landscape is burnt and hauntingly bleak. There has been no volcanic activity here for 500,000 years, though eruptions have occurred elsewhere on the island, the last in 1909 on

Island neighbours

The nearest island to Tenerife is La Gomera 30km (18 miles) west. Gran Canaria, capital of the eastern isles, is 60km (36 miles) southeast, and the sea between them is 2,000m (6,560ft) deep.

The road to Masca

Formations at Cumbre Dorsal

Montaña Chinyero, near Santiago del Teide. Lava fields created by the volcanoes are only part of a diversity of landscapes on an island the shape of an inverted triangle of just 2,034 sq km (785 sq miles). It includes tropical gardens, misty forests, fertile mountain slopes, tranquil villages, rocky headlands and black beaches, the most popular of which have been lined with imported Sahara sand.

Climate

The climate on Tenerife is pleasant all year round, with little variation in the average annual temperature of around 22°C (72°F). It is this attractive climate that has made the Canaries such a popular holiday destination. The Teide massif effectively divides Tenerife into two climatic zones, north and south.

The northerly trade winds result in more cloud cover and rainfall in the north, with the coast enjoying a constant, warm, subtropical climate. Cloud conditions constantly vary, making it sometimes hard to know what to expect. Higher up, in the cloud layer between 500 and 1,200m (1,600–4,000ft), it is cooler and more humid and the sun generally shines only in the mornings. Above the cloud layer the temperatures vary greatly between day and night; in winter they drop below freezing and snow falls, creating small lakes as it melts.

The south of the island, where the popular tourist beaches have sprung up, is hot and dry, reaching almost desert conditions. Clouds are rare and there is little rainfall, but the sirocco wind from the south occasionally causes a sandy haze called the *calima*. A steady wind on the south coast creates ideal windsurfing conditions.

Flora and Fauna

These climatic conditions and the unusual geological features have nurtured a variety of plants and wildlife, some of which are unique to the island. Comparable with Hawaii, the Galapagos and other archipelagos that have their own biodiversity, the Canary Islands as a whole have around 650 native species and nearly 40 percent of the territory is under some sort of conservation. On Tenerife 400 of the 2,000 naturally occurring plant species are endemic.

The extraordinary environment has attracted botanists down the centuries. From Germany came Alexander von Humboldt, who, in the 19th century, stopped on his way to

Bird of paradise, the Canaries' flower and a major export

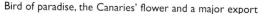

South America and gave the islands fulsome praise. The French diplomat Sabin Berthelot, an enthusiast for all things Canarian, arrived on the island in 1820 at the age of 26 and became director of the botanical gardens. From England in 1875 came Marianne North, whose works fill the gallery named after her at Kew Gardens in London.

What they found were tree-sized poinsettias, local variants of laurel and euphorbia, the *Phoenix canariensis* palm and the legendary dragon tree *(Dracaena draco)*. Among many flowers that make the island particularly attractive in May and June are the red pillars of Teide echium or 'pride of Tenerife' *(orgullo di Tenerife)* and the pink-and-white Teide broom *(Spartocytisus nubigens)*, both of which thrive in the arid Cañadas.

The island has thousands of insect species, though none is likely to do you any harm. There are grasshoppers native to each island, and the ones on Tenerife grow to 12cm (5in). Its reptiles include the Canary species of lizard, skink and gecko.

Bird Life

Many of the birds found on Tenerife will be familiar to Europeans, but there are different ones to look out for, too. Most are shy, however, and stay out of the sun, and though a variety of coloured doves are evident, don't expect to see many species as you travel around. The blue Teide finch, for example, might be seen in the National Park. Forests of Canarian pines are home to the blue chaffinch (endangered when the fires of July 2007 wiped out much of the island's pine forests, but it is hoped that breeding centres can help to restore this species' numbers) and the canary, a dull bird in the wild, which becomes yellow and more boisterous when caged (or blinded, as they once were to make them sing louder). In the scrubland you might see the Canarian pipit, Barbary partridge or Trumpeter finch. In the laurel and juniper forests look out for the Canary Island kinglet and native pigeons. Other unusual species include the collared pratincole, American golden plover, glossy ibis and Barbary falcon.

You will see ocean birds around the headlands or if you go whale- or dolphin-watching. The Canaries are on one of the principal migration routes for whales: one third of all species pass through Canarian waters each year. *(For details of birdwatching, see page 84.)*

Ecology

The island's habitat is continually under pressure, particularly from the four million tourists who arrive each year, making heavy demands on local resources. Tree felling, which began after the European conquest, has divested the island of lakes and rivers, and water is a precious commodity. Visitors should not be profligate with it. In addition, water treatment means that the taste might not always be great, so buying bottled water is both ecologically defensible and practical here.

Harnessing the trade winds

Ecology is on the mind of every islander, as ranks of new cement-block villas and apartments continue to spread over the landscape. Summer forest fires, too, have disastrous effects, often started by tourists' lack of care. Environmental protection groups are active in a place where nature is the driving cultural force.

In 2007, severe forest fires burnt out more than a third of Tenerife's forests and destroyed 900 homes. The Buenavista area and the Teno National Park were worst affected.

Population

The resident population, including 25,000 expatriates, is around 700,000, more than half living in the conurbation of Santa Cruz. In the southern resorts where most visitors go, you are likely to encounter *godos* from Galicia and other poorer regions of the Spanish mainland, who come here

Tinerfeña in a straw hat

to find work. *Tinerfeños* are cheerful, gregarious and courteous, with a love of children, parties and football. According to a folk song, 'Canarians are like the giant Teide, quiet as snow on the outside and fire in the heart'. Their carnival is, after all, one of the greatest in the world. No trace of the tall, fair-haired Guanche survives, though recent DNA sampling, using Guanche *(see page 14)* mummies, shows traces in a percentage of islanders.

The local Spanish accent is halfway between Madrid and Mexico. The 'c' and 'z' are not a lisped *th* as they are on the mainland, and consonants at the end of words sometimes fall away (examples include Santa Cru', La' Palma', and Juá instead of Juan). Some words come directly from South America (*guagua* for a bus), others from the colonial past – *chóni* for a foreigner, from the English 'Johnny' foreigner.

Isle of dogs

The native island dog is the Verdino. Smooth-haired and powerful, it weighs 40–50kg (90–110lb) and gets its name from its colour, which is slightly greenish. There is a theory that the islands were named after the native dogs (*canes* in Latin) found here in classical times.

Economy

Tourism is the main occupation of the islanders today. Agriculture is on the wane and some of the more remote villages have become abandoned. Since the conquest the island has had a series of monocultures, from sugar to bananas and cochineal. Bananas are still one of the main crops, along with tomatoes and cut flowers, particularly the bird of paradise flower *(strelitzia)*. Wine making is limited to domestic consumption.

There are no mineral resources on the island, and no industry. Its ports have suffered with the decades-long shipping decline. Because produce and manufactured goods have to be shipped in, the cost of living tends to be higher than in mainland Spain.

Government

The Canary Islands are one of the autonomous regions of Spain and a member of the European Union. Santa Cruz de Tenerife is the administrative capital of the western islands and Las Palmas on Gran Canaria the capital of the eastern islands. The presidency, which coincides with local elections, rotates between the two capitals every four years. The 60-member parliament meets in the parliament building in Santa Cruz, while the Supreme Court sits in Las Palmas.

A BRIEF HISTORY

La Orotava Valley behind Puerto de la Cruz on the north coast of Tenerife is the most fertile and pleasant on the island. When the Hispanic conquerors arrived in the 15th century they found the Taoro living here, the richest of nine island tribes, whose chief or *mencey* was called Tanasú. These tall, fair-skinned, blue-eyed people called Guanches somehow reached the Canary Islands in the 1st or 2nd century BC from northwest Africa, and were related to Berbers. They developed a written language, which remains largely undeciphered, and were ruled through councils called *tagorors*, with their court in Adeje on the west coast.

The island provided natural shelter with many caves (in Chinameda and Fasnia caves are still used today), which they decorated, and they built stone huts, too.

Guanche Culture

Not surprisingly, the volcanic giant of El Teide was central to worship for the Guanches. Their culture can be glimpsed through their funerary rites and in particular their mummifying rituals, which are explained at the Museo de la Naturaleza y el Hombre in Santa Cruz. They probably worshipped the sun, and the ancient 'pyramids' that the Norwegian explorer Thor Heyerdahl revealed in 1990 in Güímar are convincing evidence of how their ritual buildings may have looked.

The Guanches built no boats, nor did the wheel occur to them, but they were

Mysterious journey

The Guanches were, it is supposed, related to the Berbers, but how they reached the Canary Islands from Africa is a mystery. The Romans arrived to find that the islanders did not possess boats.

Guanche group, from Pueblochico near Puerto de la Cruz

adept potters, making their finest vessels for religious purposes and storing grain. Pottery and cultivation was women's work. Men hunted and tended the animals. A lack of metal ore on the island left the Guanches stuck in the stone age, with blunt instruments sharpened by bones and black volcanic obsidian, found in the Cañadas.

For food, they hunted wild cats and pigs, Barbary partridges and quail. They also kept pigs, sheep and, principally, goats, whose skins were the material of the 'loose cassocks' that they wore. But it was as a land of dogs that the island group may have been given its name. In the 1st century AD Pliny wrote of an expedition to the islands by King Juba II of Mauretania, who apparently saw many dogs roaming there. *Canis* is the Latin for dog, hence Canary Islands. The islands were fixed on the earliest classical maps as the '*Insulae Fortunatae*', the Fortunate Islands, and were the furthest western point of the known world.

The Conquest

Spanish cartographers properly mapped the islands at the end of the 14th century when the name Tenerife (actually 'Tenerifiz') appeared for the first time. The Genoese Lanzarotto Malocello is generally thought to have led the first European expedition to the Canaries, landing in the 1330s on the island that bears his name. Within a few decades conquest of the islands began. Jean de Béthencourt, a Norman adventurer employed by Henri III of Castile, made the initial advances, capturing the eastern isles and then, in 1405, El Hierro, smallest of the western isles. Tenerife, the most populous of the islands, was still in Guanche hands in 1492 when Christopher Columbus stopped at neighbouring Gran Canaria and La Gomera on his way to the New World (noting, as he did so, an eruption of El Teide, and recording that his crew thought it a sign that they should turn back).

Missionary's Betrayal

That same year, Alfonso Fernandez de Lugo, a mercenary backed by Genoese merchants, seized La Palma, following a six-year campaign against Gran Canaria. Only Tenerife remained in native hands. The influence of the conquerors of the other islands had spread to Tenerife and de Lugo's way was paved by the missionary activities of a native woman convert and lay preacher, Francisca de Gazmira. On the coast de Lugo easily defeated local tribes, moving to the better defended interior where he tricked chief Tanasú of the

Guanche cult of the dead

Taoro tribe with a sham parley. Finally, however, he was caught in a trap at Barranco de Acentejo (now the town of La Matanza, the slaughter) 16km (10 miles) into the Orotava Valley.

De Lugo escaped to return to the island with a larger force the following year and win a decisive victory on the plains of La Vitoria de Acentejo, a couple of miles south of his earlier defeat. Some 2,000 Guanches were cut down by the sophisticated Spanish crossbow, and Tanasú, the last chief of the Taoro, committed suicide.

De Lugo established his capital at San Cristóbal de la

Guanche chief

Laguna in the middle of the fertile Valle de Aguere, in striking distance of both the north and east coasts. Here the statue of Jesus that he had brought to the island came to rest in the Santuario del Cristo, and the flag that had claimed Tenerife for Spain was subsequently hung in the town hall. Santa Iglesia cathedral, which was founded ten years later in 1515, became de Lugo's resting place.

The effect of the conquerors on the local population was disastrous. The new diseases they brought spread among the Guanche population and many were taken into slavery, though the nobles were accorded due respect, and some of them intermarried. From the thousands that had inhabited the island, soon only a few hundred remained. The investors in de Lugo's expedition were rewarded with plots of land in the west, where sugar cane was introduced and refineries built at Realejos, Duate and Icod. To fuel the new economy de Lugo continued to seek Italian finance, and Portuguese were imported to harvest the canes on a share-cropping basis.

Sugar and Wine

The landscape began to change, too. Mills were stoked with timber cut from the forests, which had the long-term effect of reducing rainfall and drying up lakes, streams and springs.

Canarian sugar could not compete with that being planted in the New World, and by the end of the 15th century vineyards of the Malvasía grape had been established on the east of the island, and it was wine that offered an alternative economy as the sugar trade slumped. The grape produced sweet, dessert wines that travelled well and were particularly enjoyed by northern Europeans. By the time Shakespeare's Falstaff and Sir Toby Belch were downing 'cups of Canary', and Bostonians were talking of 'the Isles of Wine', it had become the major export.

The Canary Islands benefited from being on the trade route to the New World, and ships regularly visited Tenerife's excellent harbours, principally Garachico on the north coast, carrying sugar and slaves. Trade between Spain and the New World was confined to Spanish nationals, so smuggling and piracy became part of daily life. But in 1610 the Spanish government relaxed this restriction and foreign capitalists headed for Tenerife. By the mid-century the island had 1,500 English and Dutch residents out of a population of 50,000.

'Noble savages'

As the Guanches died out, writers romanticised them as 'noble savages'. The Spanish dramatist Félix Lope de Vega (1562–1635) created for them an idyll a long way from reality.

San Cristóbal de la Laguna, the island's first capital

The Rise of Puerto de la Cruz

Malvasía's rival was Madeira, from the Portuguese island of the same name, and when England sided with Portugal in the War of the Spanish Succession (1701–14) a major market was lost. But for another century Tenerife remained the islands' major wine producer, and the wealth that it brought paid for the rich architecture of wine towns such as Orotava. In 1706, when a volcanic eruption devastated Garachico, Puerto de la Cruz (then Puerto de la Orotava) became the island's main port.

A university was founded in La Laguna at the start of the 18th century and an intelligentsia flourished among the 70,000 *tinerfeños*. But prosperity did not survive the century and the wine trade diminished. Global conflict, with both America's War of Independence and the Napoleonic wars, during which Admiral Nelson blockaded Santa Cruz, was harmful to trade. Hardship was compounded by revolutions in Latin America, where many Canarians had gone to seek their fortunes, and payments to the families left behind were disrupted. The Canaries were themselves not without revolutionary fervour, and in 1819 the local junta put forward the islanders' desire to 'get rid of all the Spaniards now here and to put the people of this land in their place'.

Beetles to Bananas

After trade in wine had slumped, the cochineal beetle was introduced from Mexico, mainly in the eastern isles. This had a brutalising effect on the landscape as native trees were replaced by cactus for the beetle to feed on. The crop went into decline when synthetic dyes were introduced in the late 19th century, by which time bananas, said to have been introduced by the French consul, Sabin Berthelot, were making money.

In 1822 Santa Cruz had become the official capital of the archipelago and 30 years later each island was granted free

Banana workers, 1920

trade status for one of its ports, though Tenerife had two: Puerto de la Cruz and Santa Cruz, which then had the archipelago's only first-class road, to La Orotava.

Tenerife's superiority took a knock in 1881 when a harbour improvement scheme for Las Palmas on Gran Canaria eclipsed Santa Cruz.

When refrigeration arrived at the end of the 19th century, tourists came, too, on the fruit boats. To cater for them the Grand Hotel Taoro in Puerto de la Cruz was built in 1892, and for many years it was the largest hotel in Spain.

The Civil War

The Spanish Second Republic of 1931 brought new hopes of autonomy but General Franco's uprising of 1936 put paid to any such aspirations for more than 40 years. Suspected of plans against the Republican government, Franco had been sent to Tenerife in March to put him out of harm's way. From here, however, he flew from Las Palmas to the Spanish North African enclave of Melilla on 18 July. Two days later the uprising that led to the civil war was under way and the islands were in Franco's hands – La Palma was shelled by the navy before being overcome. On Tenerife, Lt Gonzales Campos was the only officer to oppose the uprising and he was shot, along with the civil governor. Republican prisoners and suspects were herded into Fyffes' banana warehouse, near Santa Cruz football ground, and shot in batches. Friend of Hitler and Mussolini, Franco was ostracised by the rest of the world until the early 1950s when Spain was welcomed back into the international community in exchange for accepting Nato bases.

Tourism and the Post-Franco Years

Tourism, the new monoculture

After Franco's death in 1975, King Juan Carlos restored democracy. Three years later a new Constitution granted degrees of autonomy to the country's regions, including the Canary Islands.

Tourism had already begun with a vengeance in Tenerife, after direct flights to the island started in 1959. Pressure on Puerto de la Cruz to build more hotels caused people within the area to sell up and transfer their plantations to the dry south, piping water into the region and opening up the barren lands in Adeje and Arona. On this coast, tourists in search of a tan flocked to the port of Los Cristianos. And this is where the boom really happened, sprawling up into Playa de las Américas, which was created in 1978, the same year that the nearby airport of Reina Sofia opened. The south of the island has been inundated with tourists ever since, and resorts continue to spread along the coast, boosting the island's economy.

The island has also become the first port of call for West African immigrants seeking a better life in Europe. In recent years thousands of exhausted migrants have washed up on the island's tourist-thronged beaches after perilous voyages in open boats. The island faced another problem in July 2007, when forest fires burnt out thousands of hectares in the west. Animals and plants were badly affected and thousands of people had to be evacuated from their homes. Fortunately, no lives were lost and the region is now recovering.

Historical Landmarks

c. 3000BC Settlers arrive from Africa.

206BC Guanches reach the island.

1st century AD Classical writers describe the islands on the edge of the known world populated by dogs (*canis*, hence Canaries).

1st–13th centuries Guanche society develops under tribal chiefs.

1440s Jean de Béthencourt, a Norman adventurer, captures the island of Hierro but fails to take Tenerife.

1492 Christopher Columbus witnesses eruption of Mt Teide en route to discovering the Americas.

1495 Tanasú, the last chief of the Taoro, commits suicide when Tenerife is conquered by Alfonso Fernandez de Lugo at the Battle of Acentejo. De Lugo introduces sugar mills.

17th century Wine replaces sugar as the main product.

1656 Sixteen Spanish galleons bringing gold from the Americas are sunk in Santa Cruz harbour by the British under Admiral Blake.

1701–14 The Canaries' university founded in La Laguna.

1706 Mount Teide erupts, destroying the main port of Garachico.

1797 Admiral Nelson's attack on Santa Cruz repelled.

1810 The first appeals for independence from Madrid.

1822 Santa Cruz becomes the capital of the archipelago.

1850–1900 Large scale emigration to Latin America.

1880s Bananas introduced.

1892 Grand Hotel Taoro, the largest in Spain, built in Puerto de la Cruz.

1927 The Canaries are divided into two provinces, with Santa Cruz administering the four western islands.

1936 General Franco launches his rebellion from Tenerife.

1959 First direct flights to Tenerife bring a new wave of tourists.

1978 The Canaries become autonomous within Spain.

1995 Spain becomes a full member of the European Union.

2002 The euro replaces the peseta as the currency of Spain.

2006 Sharp rise in the number of illegal immigrants from Africa.

2007 Severe forest fires strike the west of the island.

WHERE TO GO

Because the island is not large, it is easy to make forays from any base. Nowhere is far away, as cruise-ships passengers discover when, docking in Santa Cruz with just four hours ashore, they find they have enough time for a coach to take them to the top of El Teide and back, stopping off at La Orotava for some souvenirs, or even to hire a car and make their own way up to the cable car at the summit.

For much of the island you don't need a car. Buses are regular and inexpensive. From the capital, Santa Cruz, you can have a day out on the opposite coast in Puerto de la Cruz, the north coast resort, stopping off at the UNESCO World Heritage Site of La Laguna, with enough time to enjoy both places at leisure and return later in the day. From Los Cristianos and Playa de las Américas in the south, you can have a day out in these places, too. A hire car of course adds convenience and allows you to stop to photograph a view or to inspect the flowers, or to take advantage of signs of honey or wine for sale.

The descriptions that follow start in Santa Cruz, and continue anti-clockwise around the island.

THE NORTHEAST

Santa Cruz de Tenerife

Tenerife's capital and principal port is on the northeastern arm of the island, facing southwest and looking towards Gran Canaria, its rival, an hour's jet-foil ferry trip away. The city doesn't have a real heart, a municipal or cathedral square, but the main action takes place on the pedestrianised streets and

Playa de las Teresitas, with Santa Cruz in the distance

The Cabildo Insular and post office on Plaza de España

squares leading up from the port and also on the Rambla that sweeps round the top of the town.

The extensive waterfront area comes to climax at **Plaza de España**: to the southwest are the container ports and the industrial zone, to the northeast the jacaranda-lined Avenida de Anaga passes beside the ferry port and yachting harbour. The square is undergoing a complete transformation (see <www.plaza-esp.com>) in line with a design by architects Jacques Herzog and Pierre de Mueron. The new focal point of the square will be a circular open space around a pool of water, while the rest of the area will be filled with trees. The former heart of the square, the **Monumento a los Caídos**, dedicated to the fallen Nationalists in the Civil War, is being restored and integrated into the new design.

The art-deco buildings at the southern end of the square are the post office headquarters and the **Cabildo Insular**, containing government offices and the main tourist office.

Shopping Area

Running up from the Plaza de España is **Plaza Candelaria**, where a statue of the island's patron dates from 1772. This is the start of the main pedestrianised area and the pavement cafés are a popular meeting place. **Calle del Castillo**, the principal shopping street, heads inland past the **Parlamento de Canarias**, on the right. The 1898 neoclassical building, designed by Antonio Pintor, has been augmented to include the buildings fronting Castillo, with a green metal construction on its upper floors. Calle del Castillo ends at **Plaza del General Weyler**, where the Fuente del Amor (Fountain of Love) by Achille Caresse is overlooked by the Capitanía General, the islands' military headquarters where Franco was stationed when he started the Civil War. There's a café in the southwest corner where you can sit and watch the world go by.

On the north side of Calle del Castillo is the **Plaza del Principe**, one of the town's most pleasant squares. On the square's southeast side, near the Circulo de Amistad, is the **Museo Municipal de Bellas Artes** (open Tues–Fri 10am–8pm, Sat–Sun 10am–3pm; free). The front of the building has busts of poets, philosophers and musicians. Inside is a library and, on the first and second floors, a gallery of 16th- to 20th-century paintings. These include a panoramic picture of the foundation of Santa Cruz by Alonso de Lugo in 1494, two years after he had taken the island, and among portraits of local aristocracy is one of the French consul and botanist Sabin Berthelot who did so much for the island's plant life.

Record carnival

Santa Cruz entered the *Guinness World Records* when a record crowd of a quarter of a million filled the Plaza de España for the 1987 carnival. The Tenerife carnival is one of the biggest in Europe.

Behind the museum is the **Iglesia de San Francisco**, founded in 1680 and part of a former convent where concerts sometimes take place.

The Oldest Church

La Concepción

Eight years after Santa Cruz was founded, the town's first chapel was built where the city's main church, **Nuestra Señora de la Concepción** stands today, just to the southwest of the Cabildo Insular. The cross that de Lugo brought ashore is among its treasures. In 1652 the church was rebuilt after a fire, its octagonal tower acting as a look-out point. The lovely balcony on its exterior, a feature of church architecture throughout the island, gives its southwest front a domestic appearance. Inside, the space is cool and impressive and the beautiful coffered *mudéjar* style ceiling is also typical of the island.

In the streets around the church are some of the oldest buildings in Santa Cruz and they have been attractively maintained in warm earth colours. Stop for a drink in J.C. Murphy's in the little church square, or join the arty crowd in Tasca El Porrón further up Calle Dominguez Alfonso. This area comes alive at night, with busy cafés and bars open until the early hours. Where Calle Dominguez Alfonso meets Puente General Serrador there is a small square where evening concerts are held.

If you are strolling here in the evening, you may be lucky to chance on street theatre in which performers use the doors and balconies of the houses to put on their entertainments.

Nearby is the **Teatro Guimerá**, named after the playwright Ángel Guimerá, who was born in Santa Cruz in 1849, and made his name in Barcelona with *Terra Baixa* in 1896. La Recova, the 1851 building next to the theatre, has been housing **El Centro de Fotografía 'Isla de Tenerife'** until its move to the **Instituto Óscar Domínguez de Arte y Cultura Contemporánea**, which is under construction nearby.

Across the Barranco

From Nuestra Señora de la Concepción a bridge crosses a *barranco* (dry river bed) to the former town hospital, now the **Museo de la Naturaleza y el Hombre** (open Tues–Sun 9am–7pm; admission fee). As the name implies, all island life is here, and this is a good starting point for understanding Tenerife in all its geographical and historical aspects. Set out on three floors around two courtyards, it swarms with

Círculo de Amistad

schoolchildren in term-time, but is large enough to allow you to browse in peace. The island's flora and fauna are fully explained, as is its geology, with descriptions of winds, currents and volcanoes. Man features early on, with mummified Guanches, and displays show how the indigenous population lived. At the end is a café and an excellent bookshop.

Behind the museum, off Calle San Sebastián, is the **Mercado de Nuestra Señora de Africa**. A vibrant morning market, on two floors, shows the bounty of the island piled high, full of flowers, aromatic herbs, fruit, vegetables, meat and fish. On Sunday mornings there is a flea market, and stalls extend down Calle José Manuel Guimerá.

Auditorio and Parque Marítimo

Calle José Manuel Guimerá leads down to the main highway, Avenida del Tres de Mayo, which connects the docks to the Autopista del Norte, while the Avenida de la Constitución continues past the port towards the Autopista del Sur. The latter has become the focus of post-millennium developments with the elegant new **Auditorio** (<www.auditoriodetenerife.com>) a concert hall that is home to the Tenerife Symphony Orchestra and the place to see opera and dance. Beside it is a new bus station, and behind it, beyond

Gentlemen at War

In 1797 Admiral Nelson attacked Santa Cruz. Leading the night assault, he leapt ashore only to have his right elbow shattered by grapeshot from a cannon in the Castillo de Paso Alto. The assault was a failure but the Spanish Governor sent each captured man back to his ship with a bottle of wine and a loaf of bread. His arm amputated, Nelson returned the compliment by sending the governor cheese and a cask of beer. The captured British flags are stored in a glass case in Nuestra Señora de le Concepción.

The Auditorio, home of the Tenerife Symphony Orchestra

the old **Castillo San Juan**, is the **Parque Marítimo César Manrique** (Avenida Constitución 5; open daily 9am–5pm; admission fee), a breezy area of azure sea-water pools in imitation of the area in Puerto de la Cruz designed by the Lanzarote artist César Manrique *(see page 43)*, with trees, flowers and waterfalls. With a cafeteria and restaurant, a day out here is as good as on the beach. Beside it is a **Palmetum** with palm trees from all over the world.

The Rambla

Santa Cruz's other main avenue, the **Rambla**, meanders around the back of the town and arrives at the Avenida de Anaga, by the waterfront next to the **Museo Militar Regional de Canarias** (open Tues–Sat 10am–2pm; free). This contains some of the armour worn by the Spanish conquerors, souvenirs from Nelson's attack, including El Tigre, the cannon that shattered his right elbow *(see page 30)*, and the background to Franco's uprising in 1936. The Rambla's central pedestrian walkway, under jacaranda and Judas trees, makes it ideal for the evening *passeo* (stroll). Outdoor sculpture exhibitions have been held here since the 1970s and Henry Moore's *Goslar Warrior* is among a number of works that remain. To add to the pleasures of the Rambla, there are Chinese, Lebanese and Italian restaurants, the old Cine Victor and the bull ring, used mainly for pop concerts. The Rambla also passes the town's largest park, the 6-hectare (15-acre) **Parque García Sanabria**, which has exotic plants and a pleasant café.

The City's Beach
Avenida de Anaga continues north, following the coast past the yacht clubs from where the tycoon Robert Maxwell set sail for the last time in 1991, then towards the town's play-

Playa de las Teresitas

ground, **Playa de las Teresi-tas** (served by the No. 910 bus, which runs the 7km/ 4 miles along the waterfront every 20 minutes). Stretching 1.5km (1 mile), it's the most golden beach on the island, its imported Sahara sand lapped by shallow waters: dogs, surfboards, ball games and the hanging of towels or clothes on trees are all banned. Kiosks sell snacks, and at weekends locals en-liven the atmosphere in the restaurants, notably the Con-

Picturesque Igueste

fredí de Pescadores by the fishermen's shacks. There are more places to eat in **San Andrés**, the fishing village of the origi-nal port, where the road heads into the Anaga Hills. After 15 minutes' drive the road reaches the **Mirador de Rozasosa**, offering a last, stunning glimpse of the coast as well as walks through the glorious, herb-scented hills.

On the coast beyond Playa de las Teresitas the road winds without let-up, with the exception of the **Punta de los Organos** *mirador*, which provides a last chance to look down on the beach. A couple of kilometres further on, a turn leads down to the secluded beach of Las Gaviotas beneath the cliffs, where swimsuits are an option. The road ends at **Igueste**, an attractive cluster of white villas among terraces of mangoes and avocados, winding steeply down before com-ing to a stop several hundred metres short of a small grey beach. From here you can walk to the little beach and one-family hamlet of **Antequera**. The Rincon de Anaga is a pop-ular little family-run restaurant at the entrance to Igueste.

La Laguna

Designated the capital of Tenerife by the island's conqueror, Alonso de Lugo, **San Cristóbal de la Laguna** is visibly the most ancient town on the island, with mansions dating from the 15th century. It is generally known simply as La Laguna, but the lagoon which it was once sited on and named after has long since disappeared. The town, a World Heritage Site, is at the centre of a large agricultural district, and is a cradle of learning and religion, with a university and bishop's see.

Just inland from Santa Cruz, La Laguna is regarded as a suburb of the capital, but in the 20 minutes or so that it takes to reach it, the climate can noticeably cool, and you should be prepared with warmer clothing. The old part of town, the *casco histórico*, is on a grid system, and the starting point of a visit should be the **Plaza del Adelantado**. The municipal market, at the far end of the square, is undergoing restoration

Intricately carved balcony, La Laguna

and has been temporarily re-housed in a modern hall just beyond. The town is popular with visitors from the capital on Saturdays and Sundays, when parking is difficult and the square's bars are buzzing. On the opposite side of the

> **Taking the tram**
>
> A new tram service linking La Laguna with Santa Cruz opened in 2007, running on old tram lines that were last used in 1957. See <www.tranviatenerife.com> for timetables and prices.

square are a trio of impressive but disparate buildings. To the left is the neoclassical **Ayuntamiento** (town hall), which contains the flag that de Lugo planted when he arrived from Spain. To the right is the **Palacio de Nava**, a baroque mansion that belonged, in the early 18th century, to the Marquis de Villanueva del Prado, whose glittering salon attracted the thinkers of the day. He was also responsible for establishing the Botanic Garden in La Orotava. In between is the massive **Iglesia-Convento de Santa Catalina de Siena**, with a 'Canarian' balcony on the corner from where the nuns can glimpse the outside world.

Calle Obispo Rey Redondo leads along the blank wall of the convent, past three 17th-century mansions, which make this the most impressive corner of town. The tourist office is housed in the Casa de Alvaredo Bracamonte (open daily 9am–5pm). Wander down this street to the **Catedral**, where de Lugo is buried behind the altar, and the **Iglesia de la Concepción**, which dates from 1502. Its font was used to baptise converted Guanche leaders. In Calle San Agustin it is possible to see the interior of a mansion, at Casa Lercaro, home to the **Museo de Historia** (open Tues–Sun 9am–7pm; admission fee, Sundays free; <www.museosdetenerife.org>). This fine building, with its own small chapel, was built by the Genoan Lercaro family of bankers in 1593, the owner's first son, Francisco, becoming the Lt-Governor of Tenerife. The building is an ideal setting to lay out five centuries of the island's history.

La Laguna locals

From the Plaza del Adelantado, Calle Nava de Grimón leads past the peach-coloured walls of the **Convento de Santa Clara de Asis**, the town's other immense convent, to the Convent of San Miguel de las Victorias Franciscanes. Here, the **Santuario del Santísimo Cristo de La Laguna** contains a figure of Christ commissioned by de Lugo from a Flemish sculptor in 1520. Dripping with New World silver and gold, it is the town's most venerated figure.

Two major museums are within reach of La Laguna. On the outskirts of the town is the **Museo de la Ciencia y el Cosmos** (Calle Via Láctea s/n; open Tues–Sun 9am–7pm; admission fee, Sundays free). This hands-on museum is an introduction to cosmology and the planets. The other is the excellent **Museo de Antropología de Tenerife** in the Casa de Carta in Valle de Guerra (Carretera Tacoronte-Valle de Guerra s/n; open Tues–Sun 9am–7pm; admission fee, Sundays free). This museum of popular culture is beautifully laid out, and depicts five centuries of rural life on the island.

The fertile Valle de Guerre is a centre for flower growing. Looking down on it is the **Mirador de El Boquerón**, where a map shows the distribution of agriculture, of bananas, avocados, potatoes, vines and the bird of paradise flower, which has become a symbol of the islands.

To the east, beyond the villages of **Tegueste** and **Tejina**, is **Bajamar**, a small, old-fashioned resort where people from La Laguna come to soak in the sea-water pools. Beyond it is

Punto Hidalgo, a good place for coastal walks, which are signposted from the roundabout at the end of the town. The flower-covered Café Melita on the way into Punto Hidalgo has wonderful cakes and pastries, and views over the sea.

The Anaga Hills

The best view of La Laguna is from the **Mirador Jardín** in the **Monte de las Mercedes**. Looking down on the town and both coasts, it has a helpful explanation of where the lagoon was and how it gradually faded away. Listen for canaries in the trees and bushes. You might glimpse one, but they are not as bright in the wild as they are in captivity.

Las Mercedes forest is the start of the **Montañas de Anaga**, a series of volcanic hills rising to about 1,000m (3,300ft) with deep valleys running down to the sea, ending in small beaches accessible only by boat or after hours of walking. The best place to begin is beyond the Jardín at a second mirador, **Cruz del Carmen** at 920m (3,018ft), though the thickets of heather and fern give less of a view. The visitor centre (open daily 9.30am–3pm in summer, until 4pm in winter) for the **Parque Rural Anaga** is here. There is a small exhibition about the natural history of the local area, and an information

The Anaga Hills

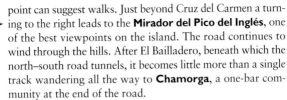

point can suggest walks. Just beyond Cruz del Carmen a turning to the right leads to the **Mirador del Pico del Inglés**, one of the best viewpoints on the island. The road continues to wind through the hills. After El Bailladero, beneath which the north–south road tunnels, it becomes little more than a single track wandering all the way to **Chamorga**, a one-bar community at the end of the road.

The road north of El Bailladero leads through **Taganana**, a community of white houses and palms, which in 1881 felt so cut off it declared itself independent. Its 15th-century church is one of the oldest on the island. Beyond it is **Playa San Roque**, where surfers gather on the small beach in front of the buzzy Bar Playa Casa Africa. Further on is a string of restaurants at **Roques de las Bodegas**, and at **Benijo** the road dissolves into paths heading over the cliffs.

The dense vegetation of these hills includes the largest natural laurel forest in the Canary Islands, their leaves often dripping with moisture from the misty climate produced by the Trade Winds. Their prehistoric ecosystem supports bay trees, holly, heather and spurge, while the damp climate keeps alive the ferns, lichen and moss. There are also a number of cave houses here, such as those at **Chinamada**, where one of them has been turned into a bar and restaurant called La Cueva.

Walking in the Anaga Hills

Walking is the best way to explore the Anaga Hills. A starting point is the Visitor Centre at Cruz del Carmen, or the Albergue Montes de Anaga (see page 127), where you can obtain maps of the *senderos* (paths). Several walks begin around Las Carboneras, including one down to the sea at Punto Hidalgo, passing through three identifiable ecosystems. A more dramatic walk is from Chamorga at the end of the road down to Faro de Anaga, the lighthouse on the northeastern tip.

THE NORTH COAST

The fertile Orotava Valley made the Guanche tribe here the wealthiest on the island. It did the same for the colonisers who made the most of the ideal growing conditions, building impressive mansions on the proceeds. Villa Orotava, as La Orotava was then called, was a gateway up to El Teide. Just below it, where the valley arrived at the sea, was Puerto de la Orotava, a handy port from where wine and other products could be shipped abroad. But in 1706 a volcanic eruption destroyed the north coast's major port of Garachico. Overnight Puerto de la Orotava's fortunes increased, and the port was re-named Puerto de la Cruz as a sign that it would do business with the whole island. When tourism started, this part of the island was where the curious visitors came, for the climate, the Botanic Gardens, the architecture and for

The coast around Puerto de la Cruz beneath El Teide

Playa Jardín, Puerto de la Cruz

El Teide. By then Alexander Humboldt had paid a visit and made his pronouncements. A mirador between La Orotava and Puerto de la Cruz marks the spot where the German naturalist expressed his delight in the view, though he was not so delighted when he returned from his trip up to El Teide to discover that his porters had abandoned the plant and mineral samples he had collected, because they thought them unnecessary ballast. It was not long before other botanists and natural philosophers were making the journey up the mountain, followed by the first holidaymakers, and when the Grand Hotel Taoro was built in 1892 it was the largest in Spain.

Puerto de la Cruz

The island's oldest resort has a population of 32,000 and a gentle air, with handsome buildings, a small fishermen's quarter and a romantic seafront. Gently lit at night, the promenade wanders beneath palm trees, beside black rocks and beaches where white-crested waves pound reassuringly. From the black beaches of Playa Jardín to Playa Martiánez and beside the tropical oasis of Lago Martiánez, it is a delight at any time of the day. The heart of the town is just inland from the harbour around the **Plaza del Charco de los Camarones**, named after a pool full of shrimps, that was once here. There are café tables, kiosks, bands and the general hum of the town's life.

On the east side Calle Quintana leads to the 16th-century **Ermita de San Juan Baptista** and the 18th-century **Iglesia de San Francisco**, effectively one church with the dividing wall removed. They contain a medley of paintings of the Madonna. The area opposite is used for staging concerts and other cultural events.

The street continues up past two handsome mansions with elegant patios and balconies, now the hotels **Monopol** and **Marquesa** (see page 130). The Monopol, dating from 1742, was the birthplace of Agustín de Bethencourt y Molina, founder of the Madrid Civil Engineers' School and General Director of Ports and Roads for Alexander II of Russia. The Marquesa, more elegant still, has pavement tables that are ideal for people-watching. In front of them the street opens into the Plaza de la Iglesia and the town's principal church, **Iglesia de Nuestra Señora de la Peña de Francia**, built in 1697 with a tower added in 1898. The organ was made in London.

The Harbour

The harbour today is small with little activity, and it is hard to imagine it as a stopping point for transatlantic trade. On the eastern side is the distinctive **Casa de la Aduana**, the former customs house and residence of the royal tax collector (open Mon–Sat 10am–8pm; free). Part of the house now contains Puerto de la Cruz's main **tourist office** and another houses an artesanal craft shop. To the west is **La Ranilla**, the fishermen's quarter, where the seafront

Plaza Galdós

Plaza Pérez Galdós, named after the Spanish playwright and novelist who was born in Gran Canaria in 1843, is the most pleasant square in La Ranilla. Stop here for a drink or *tapas* at one of the small restaurants or bars.

Toucan at Loro Parque

has been waiting a considerable time for the development of some kind of park. Because of the potential damage from the Atlantic, land directly on the seafront is not always regarded as a prime building site. On La Ranilla's Calle El Lomo there's a small Archaeological Museum of Guanche ceramics (open Tues–Sat 10am–1pm and 5–9pm, Sun 10am–1pm; admission fee). At the far end of La Ranilla, beyond the football ground and municipal swimming pool, is the 17th-century **Castillo San Felipe**, sometimes used for exhibitions. It marks the start of the town's main black beach, **Playa Jardín**, which is attractively landscaped behind. At the far end of the beach is Punta Brava and **Loro Parque** (open daily 8am–5pm, last exit 6.45pm; admission fee; <www.loroparque.com>), one of the island's big attractions, with killer whale, dolphin and sea lion shows, an aquarium, an orchidarium and what is claimed to be the largest collection of parrots in the world.

The Promenade

On the eastern side of the port, behind the customs house, is the **Plaza de Europa**, a fake castle with genuine cannons, built in 1992 on top of a very handy central car park. The streets behind the square are thick with handsome 18th- and 19th-century mansions with fine doorways and balconies. These lead to the promenade beside the small, rocky San Telmo beach where pools have been cut in the rocks for swimmers. The little white **San Telmo chapel**, dedicated to the patron saint of seamen, was built in 1780 on the site of a coastal battery.

On the point of land beyond here is the enchanting **Lago Martiánez** (open daily 9.30am–7pm; admission fee), one of the great attractions of the town. With palms, boulders and sky-blue swimming pools, this wonderful area compensates for a lack of really good natural swimming facilities in the town. It was designed by César Manrique (1919–92), the artist from Lanzarote who did so much to promote the islands' natural resources. It is easy to spend a whole day in the complex, which has a café and restaurant, and thanks to a new casino you can spend the evening here too.

The promenade, where Africans braid hair and sell carvings, bags and other leather goods, opens up as it reaches **Playa Martiánez**, the town's other beach that looks towards the cliffs rising to the east.

Lago Martiánez, designed by Canarian artist César Manrique

Jardín Botánico

At the back of the town is the **Jardín Botánico** (open daily 9am–7pm, 6pm in winter; admission fee; <www.icia.es>), properly known as Jardín de Aclimatación de la Orotava. It started life in 1788 as a staging post between the New World and Europe, allowing tropical and sub-tropical plants to become used to cooler temperatures. The pamphlet that comes with your entry ticket gives a layout of the garden and its species. As a scientific institute, it is especially dedicated to the flora of the Canary Islands, with more than 30,000 specimens.

The **Parque Taora**, a landscape of gardens and ponds around the **Casino Taora**, is also a botanic delight.

Just beyond the Botanic Garden is the **Ábaco Casa Museo**, a beautiful 18th-century country house reconstructed with period furniture and a bounteous kitchen. Visits include a show of Canarian song and dance, plus a video. The bar and restaurant are open in the evenings.

Further diversions include the **Bananera El Guanche** tropical farm (open daily 9am–6pm; admission fee; a free bus runs from Hotel Atlantis). This gives an insight into the island's agriculture; fruit and plants are on sale. **Oasis del Valle** (open daily 10am–5pm; admission fee) is another jaunt by exit 33 of the motorway, offering donkey and camel rides, a zoo and botanic garden. **Pueblochico** (open daily 9am–7pm in summer, 9am–6pm in winter; admission fee; <www.pueblochico.com>) by exit 35 is a small park with some of the island's buildings in miniature. Free buses run to both attractions from Avenida Venezuela.

La Orotava

The historic centre of Tenerife's most attractive town is unsign-posted, and visitors by car may find themselves going round in circles before they make it right up to the top right-hand side of the town where the island's wealthy landowners and merchants built their mansions. **La Orotava** is high above sea level and its streets are steep. Follow the 'Parking San Agustín' signs. Once you arrive, however, sites are helpfully marked and a useful tourist map is available at the tourist office.

The church of **San Agustín**, which belonged to a former monastery, has a beautiful wood ceiling and a handsome retable. It sits at one end of the Plaza de la Constitución, which is overlooked by **Liceo de Taoro**, a grand private club, now open for the public to look around, and the adjacent **Jardínes Marquesado de la Quinta Roja**, also known as Jardin Victoria. These formal gardens were laid out in the

View from Plaza de la Constitución towards the coast

Casa de los Balcones

19th century around the mausoleum of the Marquis – membership of the Masons precluded him from a burial on consecrated ground. Wilder and more lush are the **Hijuelo del Botánico** gardens just beyond. Worth visiting, too, is the nearby **Museo de Cerámica** (Calle Leon 3; open Mon–Sat 10am–6pm, Sun 10am–4pm; admission fee) in Casa Tafuriaste, a studio and showroom with a collection of traditional Spanish ceramics.

Calle Carrera del Esculter Estévez runs along the bottom of Plaza de la Constitución and west past the town's tourist information office. This street then leads past the **Ayuntamiento** (town hall), an imposing neoclassical building which gives a clue as to how important La Orotava once was. The square in front of it is brilliantly decorated at Corpus Cristi *(see page 94)* using different coloured earth, sand and volcanic cinders.

Beyond here, the buildings give a sense of the riches that once flowed through the town. At the top of this road is the island's most famous domestic building, the 17th-century **Casa de los Balcones** (open Mon–Sat 8.30am–6.30pm, Sun 8.30am–1.30pm; <www.casa-balcones.com>) which, as its name suggests, has superlative wood balconies. For many years it has been associated with the island's lace making, and there are several other outlets on the island. Staff in traditional costume will show you the best of the island's wares. Otherwise you can explore the beautiful patio and, for a small fee, the period rooms upstairs, peopled with dummies in costume, including a granny sound asleep in her bed.

Casa del Turista, the mansion opposite Casa de los Balcones, is almost as grand, and is part of the same outlet for island ware and lace. A few metres further up on the right is the Hospital de la Santísima Trinidad. Inside the courtyard is the revolving drum on the main door via which abandoned babies would be left in the care of the hospital's nuns.

Town Church

Below these old streets is the **Iglesia de Nuestra Señora de la Concepción**, La Orotava's main church, built in the 16th century and rebuilt after devastating earthquakes in 1705, and retaining the original marble altar. Further down the hill is the **Museo de Artesanía Iberoamericana** (open Mon–Fri 9am–6pm, Sat 9am–2pm; admission fee), which has an intriguing collection of ceramics, baskets, instruments and furniture from all over Latin America.

Opposite is the 17th-century **Casa Torrehermosa** which sells a selection of crafts, backed by the local government. There are several good restaurants in and

A fertile land

'Around Orotava is the finest, most fertile land in these islands, and even in the whole of Spain, because on it can be grown and bred anything you may desire.' – Fray Alonso de Espinosa (1594)

around La Orotava, such as Sabor Canario and La Victoria, which offer further opportunities to check out the interiors of these picturesque mansions.

The Wine Lands of Tacoronte

East of Puerto de la Cruz, above the motorway on a pleasant rural road, are the villages of **La Mantanza de Acentejo** and **La Victoria de Acentejo**, scenes of the decisive battles between the Guanche *mencey* (chief), Bencomo, and the Spaniard Alonso Fernandez de Lugo. Matanza (the slaughter) is where 1,200 Spaniards were caught in a trap on 31 May, 1494. Only 200 escaped, de Lugo among them. He returned with a larger force the following year to win a decisive victory a short distance away at La Vitoria de Acentejo on Christmas Day 1495. Some 2,000 Guanche were slaughtered. It is difficult to imagine such scenes of carnage in these quiet hills.

Acres of vineyards mark this region out as **Tacoronte-Acentejo**, the best of the island's five DO wine regions *(see page 102)*. Just beyond La Matanza, the road goes under the motorway to arrive at **Casa del Vino La Baranda** (open Wed–Sat 10am–9.30pm, Sun 11am–6pm, Tues 11.30am–7.30pm in summer, 10.30am–6.30pm in winter; free; <www.cabtfe.es/casa-vino>), just before entering El Sauzal. This 17th-century estate is an attractive collection of buildings that includes a wine press and museum with detailed displays in both Spanish and English about viniculture on Tenerife. It is an impressive story, and the number of different bottles on display –

Casa del Vino, El Sauzal

San Pedro, El Sauzal

tinto, rosado and *blanco* – may come as a surprise to anyone who has been searching for a selection of Canary wines on restaurant menus. The House of Wine has its own bar and restaurant and a room for sampling and buying wine. To further delight the palate, visit the **Casa de la Miel** (House of Honey; open Tues–Sat 10am–10pm, Sun 11am–6pm; <www.casadelamiel.org>), also on the La Baranda estate and run by the island council as a centre for extracting and bottling honey.

High above the rocky coast, best seen from La Garañona mirador, **El Sauzal** is set on a slope, and the square outside the town hall teeters down attractive steps beside a waterfall. **Tacoronte**, too, is way above the sea, and as may be expected it has a number of *bodegas* and restaurants. Its historic main square, Plaza del Cristo, is overlooked by a 17th-century church and convent of the same name, and at Corpus Christi coloured earth and flowers carpet the square. Ten minutes' walk down a steep hill is the church of **Santa Catalina**, with a typical balcony. It has two of the finest retables on the island and among its paintings is a fine *Inmaculada* by José Luján Pérez. The coast at Tacoronte looks tantalisingly close, but the journey down is steep and winding. **Mesa Mar** has a small beach and bars. Just beyond, along a pleasant coast road, is **El Pris**, a small bay with fish restaurants.

West of Puerto de la Cruz

The motorway west of Puerto de la Cruz peters out at **Los Realejos**, which it divides between the older, upper part, Realejo Alto, and the lower, modern town, Realejo Bajo. This is the last chapter in the subjugation of the Guanches, where de Lugo pitched camp in 1498 and accepted the surrender of the remaining indigents and their lands. The much renovated church of Santiago Apóstol in the upper town still has the font where the converted Guanches were baptised.

Beyond Los Realejos is **San Juan de la Rambla**, an attractive small white village by the sea. Inland, high above it, is La Guancha, a quiet artesanal village with fine views.

Icod de los Vinos is on the tourist map for its dragon tree, **El Drago Milenario**. Reaching 17m (56ft) with a 6-m (20-ft) circumference, it is the largest and most ancient on the island. It stands by the main road on the west side of the town,

The Dragon Tree

The dragon tree *(Draecana draco)*, which dates from the prehistoric Tertiary period, is unique to the Canary islands. It held a mystical quality for the Guanches, who saw it as a symbol of fertility and wisdom, using its bark on their shields when they went to war. Its resin, known as dragons' blood, turned red on contact with the air, and was used to embalm the Guanche dead. In Europe other uses were found for it, to dye hair golden, to stain marble red and to varnish violins.

helped in its old age by metal and concrete supports. Hard to date, it may not be quite the 1,000 years old that it claims. Near the small park in which the tree stands is **Mariposario del Drago** (open daily 9am–6pm in winter, 9am–7pm in summer; admission fee), a tropical garden full of butterflies from all over the world.

The dragon tree at Icod

The old town of Icod is one of the most attractive on the island. Its typical buildings are best around the Plaza de Constitución, shaded by palms, oleander and jacaranda, and in Plaza de la Pila, where the 19th-century Casa de los Cáceres is used as an exhibition centre. Icod has long been the centre of a wine producing area, and you can buy its wares at the Casa del Vino in Plaza de Constitución. A wine festival takes place every year on the eve of St Andrew's Day (29 November), when locals ride on sleds down the steep streets of the town making as much noise as possible, in remembrance of the wine barrels once taken down to the port for export.

In a little square below the Plaza is the church of San Marcos, which contains a sacristy and small museum. Among its treasures is a filigree cross made of Mexican silver weighing 47kg (104lb). Pinewoods behind the town stretch up towards El Teide. On the coast **Playa San Marcos** has an attractive small black beach with fishing boats and restaurants.

EL TEIDE

The traditional path up to El Teide (it rhymes with 'lady') for early visitors to the island was from La Orotava. They would be taken by guides with mules up the track used by pumice miners and by the *neveros*, who brought ice down from the mountains to make ice cream. Today there are four main roads up to the **Parque Nacional del Teide**, so wherever you are on the island it is always accessible. The park was named a World Heritage Site by UNESCO on June 29th, 2007.

Unless you are up for a five-hour climb, the last part of the journey has to be made by the Teleférico (cable car), 1.6km (1 mile) north of the Parador hotel and 8km (5 miles) south of the Visitor Centre. It does not operate during windy weather. You should arrive early in the morning to avoid queues. The highest mountain in Spain is 3,718m (12,198ft) above sea level and it is cold. Snow caps it for most of the year and temperatures can be well below freezing point. Yet it is still surprising to learn how many of the 2.5 million people who visit the park each year turn up in beach wear.

Most people who alight from the cable car do not want to stroll far, and those who are pregnant or suffer from coronary or respiratory problems should not attempt to do so, as there is 50 percent less oxygen in the air than at sea level. It is possible to walk just beneath the crater. It is also possible to walk on its rim, but to prevent erosion from hikers' boots, the authorities have introduced a system whereby you have to have written permission to do this. Permits can be obtained free from the Parque Nacional del Teide on the fourth floor of Calle Emilio Calzadilla 5 in Santa

Cruz (tel: 922 29 01 29; open Mon–Fri 9am–2pm; <www.telefericoteide.com>). You will need to take your passport and you will also need to show your free summit permit on the mountain top.

The Cañadas

El Teide rises from a great hollow in the centre of the island, a caldera, or cooking pan, that is the remnants of an earlier, much larger volcano, of around 4,800m (16,000ft). This flat, pale expanse between the remnants of the former crater wall and the peak of El Teide forms the park. In fact there were two earlier volcanoes, creating two calderas, separated by the mauve and pink barrier of Los Roques de García. Together they form an egg-shaped area 15km (9 miles) across. Lava and ashes have spilled from the volcanoes in a series of eruptions at different times, which explains why

El Teide, Spain's highest mountain

the rocks are so varied in texture and colour. Some cooled quickly into jagged formations, others cooled slowly into smoother, more liquid shapes.

El Teide lies to the north of the park and volcanic activity continues around the parasitic cones that sprouted around it. The most recent eruptions have formed a caldera on the summit of El Teide where fumaroles – escape hatches for steam – still blow. In 1798 an eruption created Las Narices del Teide (Teide's nostrils) on the south flank. The most recent eruption from these peaks occurred in 1909 from Montaña Chinyero,

Early risers make for the summit of El Teide

which is located in the west of the park, and El Teide is considered by experts to be still active.

Pico Viejo (3,134m/10,282ft) is to the southwest of El Teide and was formed a little earlier. A number of other volcanic peaks rise from the solidified lava in the park. To the north are the large caves of Cueva del Hielo or Cueva de los Cazadores. The highest point on the rim is Guajara (2,717m/ 8,914ft) on the south side of the Parador, and beyond it is the Paisaje Lunar, a haunting lunar landscape. Around Guajara Pass, which once linked the Orotava road with Vilaflor, are former Guanche huts and many of the island's mummies have been found in caves nearby.

The Routes into the Park

Once fertile lands scattered with small lakes, the calderas were the summer pastures for the Guanches' sheep and goats. They entered the region through *cañadas*, the breaches in the rim of the calderas that give the park its name. These are most visible on the southern side where the Llano de Ucanca is the site of a former lake. The four modern roads into the park rise steeply and there are few other places on earth where the landscape changes so quickly, from lush valleys to the rocky, volcanic terrain of the higher elevations, passing through a cloud level between 1,000 and 1,500m (3,300–5,000ft).

From the North

The road that leads from La Orotava twists and climbs steeply through the moist Orotava Valley, past thatched

Climbing El Teide Peak

The path to the summit around Montaña Blanca starts approximately 2km (1 mile) east of the Teleférico (cable car) base, where there is parking space for about a dozen cars and a map of the route. It is a straight walk up, with no scrambling or climbing, and it takes about five hours, during which you will climb around 1,400m (4,600ft). You can return via the Teleférico. A fleece and waterproof jacket are recommended, and in winter you should also wear snow glasses. Camping is not allowed in the park, but there is a refuge, the Refugio de Altavista, at 3,250m (10,650ft). Just beyond the refuge is a 19th-century ice cave, where early visitors cooled themselves after the horse ride up from La Orotava.

As the path reaches the top of the Teleférico, you will need to present your permit (see page 52) and passport to a ranger before continuing along the Telesforo Bravo path to the rim of the crater, through fumaroles emitting sulphurous clouds. The view is absolutely spectacular, and on a clear day you should be able to see all of the Canary Islands.

barns and patches of agricultural land towards the village of **Aguamansa**, where there are forest trails through the pines, and aviaries in which sick or wounded birds are taken care of. The village is situated in the cloud level, so if you plan to go for a walk, be prepared for some precipitation. Nearby is **Los Organos**, rock formations that look like organ pipes. Beyond Aguamansa look for another geological curiosity on the left-hand side of the road, the **Marguerita de Piedra**, a lump of basalt rock that seems to have exploded, forming daisy-like petals. Finally, at 2,020m (6,630ft), the road is joined by the road from La Laguna and it enters the park at the Portillo Pass.

The cable car

From the East

The road from La Laguna is also the best route from Santa Cruz, so it can be busy at weekends. Built in the 1940s by the military, this road is the straightest, least steep of the four, running along the ridge of the Cumbre Dorsal and providing spectacular views over both coasts. It passes through **La Esperanza**, a place known for its roadside meat restaurants. From here the **Bosque la Esperanza**, a forest of pines and picnic spots, spreads beside the road for a dozen kilometres. On the left, before the first viewpoint at **Mirador de las Flores**, is **Las Raíces**, the spot where Franco and a hundred co-conspirators met at an out-door lunch in June 1939 to seal their agreements shortly before their attack on the mainland. A monument marks the spot.

At 2,400m (7,900ft) the road reaches two sky-watching institutions, the **Observatorio Meteorológico de Izaña** and the **Observatorio Astronómico del Teide**. Increasing light pollution on the island has affected the usefulness of the observatory (tel: 922 60 52 00; open to the public by appointment only).

The Starting Point

As the peak comes dramatically into view, the road from La Laguna meets the one from La Orotava at **El Portillo** just before the **Visitor Centre** (open daily 9am–4pm). Moroccan cedars have been introduced here as part of an attempt to replant deforested areas. Measures to conserve the nature of the park have meant that many paths are closed to vehicles and hikers. Essential maps and guides should be on sale here, but don't count on them being in stock: if you are walking, it is best to try to find decent maps before reaching the park. Videos and displays give a good grounding into the history of the park and an idea of what to expect. Some tours and guides are advertised or may be available. You can check out the flora here: Teide daisies flower in the winter snow, pink broom blossoms in May, the Teide violet a little later. The rock's colour depends on the time of day and the light: the lava is in extraordinary hues of yellows, reds and browns, and there's the shiny black obsidian with which the Guanche made blades for their tools and weapons.

Cable Car and Parador

From the Visitor Centre it is about 12km (7 miles) to the **Teleférico** or cable car. It runs up the mountain from 9am to 4pm (with the last chance to come down again at 5pm),

View from the top

takes eight minutes, and stops 170m (560ft) short of the summit. Refreshments are available at both the top and bottom. Paths from the top lead to two miradors at the foot of the final ascent, for which you need a permit *(see page 52)*. From the viewpoints you can see the jagged rocky and rope-like formations from the mountain's latest lava flows.

The **Parador de Cañadas del Teide** *(see page 129)* is the only hotel in the park and it makes an excellent base for an early start to walk to the summit. The night sky is sparkling, and groups of visitors come to the Parador for dinner and astronomical talks. Near the Parador are **Los Roques de García**, extraordinary gnarled formations that are all that is left of the dividing wall between the two former volcanoes that make up the caldera. They are among the most photographed phenomenon in the park. Stones near these rocks are deep green from copper oxide, and are known as **Los Azulejos**, the glazed tiles.

From the Southwest

From Playa de las Américas, Los Cristianos and the other resorts of the southwest, the 90-minute drive up to the park starts either at Arona or at Granadilla de Abona and climbs steeply to where the roads converge at **Vilaflor**. Situated at an altitude of 1,400m (4,600ft), this village is the highest in Spain, and its population of 2,000 makes it the island's smallest municipality. It stands among volcanic cones in the middle of pine woods, of which the Pino Gordo, the fat pine, is the finest example, 65m (215ft) tall and 10m (30ft) in circumference. Vilaflor is a good base for exploring the mountains and is the nearest village to the park, where there are no shops or commercial outlets. Its 16th-century church was founded by a Catalan colonialist, Pedro Soler, who first put this land to work for the Spanish. Vilaflor is a popular stopping point, so if you wish to stay here, try to book a hotel in advance.

It is noticeably cooler here than on the coast and it snows in winter. Generally, however, when the weather is poor on the coast, it is sunny up here above the clouds. The bare earth on the tidy, geometrical terraces is covered with lava pebbles called *picón*, which help to hold in the moisture. There is no shortage of water, and underground springs provide the island with bottled water. There is enough moisture for a healthy agricultural industry of tomatoes, potatoes and grapes. These must be among the highest vineyards in the world and their white wines are increasingly talked about.

Roques de García

Alpine flowers

Just outside Vilaflor is the **Ermita San Roque** with a mirador and the Restaurant El Mirador, which makes a good stopping place. There are two further miradors beside the road, **Mirador de las Pinos** and just beyond a large bottling plant, **Mirador las Lajas**. Both make pleasant picnic stops.

From the West

The road from the west coast rises from the white village of **Chio**, at 680m (2,240ft), from where there is a panoramic view back over the coast around the high cliffs of Los Gigantes. Less twisting than the road through Vilaflor, it climbs through the inhospitable, jagged clinker and dark grey lava to reach the road from Vilaflor at **Boca de Tauce**. Here a breach in the caldera rim lets the road through into the lunar landscape of the park.

THE NORTHWEST

The northwest of the island is one of its richest and most diverse areas. Deeply rural, it has many hidden corners as well as popular spots, none of which is ever very crowded. Much of the area is covered by **El Teno Rural Park**, a conservation area of more than 80sq km (30sq miles) based on the Teno massif, one of the geologically oldest parts of the island. There is a range of vegetation between the hills and valleys, and wild flowers are in abundance. Bird life is also very active, both in the hills and around the northern coastal plain, and sea birds can be seen from Punto El Teno. **Isla Baja** is the name given to the region that covers the districts of Buenavista, Garachico, Los Silos and El Tanque. Its capital is Garachico, which makes a good base. A number of traditional houses and *fincas* (country estates) throughout the region have been converted into places to stay.

Garachico

An hour before dawn on 5 May 1709, the sky above **Garachico** was lit up by the eruption of El Volcán Negro, 8km (5 miles) inland. It was not long before two streams of lava were scorching their way through forests and vineyards towards the coast. Alarmed, the people of Garachico, Tenerife's main port, watched it coming. Genoese merchants abandoned their mansions and monks and nuns left their religious houses, fleeing the path of the boiling lava. In the harbour, ships trading in sugar and wine could only put to sea and watch as the river of molten earth barged and burned its way through the town's buildings and filled up the harbour, turning the sea to a boiling cauldron. Garachico's days of glory were over, and it would never be the same again.

If you go up to the **Mirador de Garachico** you can look down on the white

Castillo de San Miguel, Garachico

buildings that cover the curve of lava jutting out into the sea and make out the paths of the two devastating rivers of molten rock. In the town itself there is a model of the catastrophe in the Isla Baja restaurant.

Garachico today is a handsome town of 6,000 that is so unhurried that it needs no traffic lights. Its seafront is given over to leisure, with a municipal pool (now being restored) and a football pitch. Once or twice a year the sea comes in and batters the pitch, though most days the blue water looks benign, especially where it laps the black swimming rocks around the **Castillo de San Miguel**. With its bar and restaurant, this is a good place to look out across the sea as the sun sets. The castle, dating from 1570, has a collection of shells from around the world, and provides a viewing point from its battlements.

Just inland from the castle is the pretty **Plaza de Juan Gonzales de la Torre**, at the back of which the former land gate to the harbour has been excavated. There is a huge 17th-century wine press here, too, a reminder of the time when locally produced Malvasia wine made Garachico – and Tenerife – rich. Nearby is a monument to Cristóbal de Ponte, the Genoan banker who founded the town. Behind the square is El Lagar de Julio, a good local *tasca*.

Nuestra Señora de los Angeles

A few steps from the square is the parish church of **Santa Ana**. Rebuilt after the eruption, it contains a magnificent crucifix by Martin de Andujar, a Sevillian craftsman, and a figure of Christ made by Tarasco Indians in Mexico. Beside the church, the small curved Calle Esteban de Ponte follows the seafront. The de Ponte family house is located here, and impressive buildings include the Isla Baja restaurant and El Jardín *pensión*, which is op-

Doorway in Garachico

posite the tourist information office and Limonera craft shop.

The main square, Plaza de la Libertad, which remains much as it must have looked before the eruption, is shaded and has a small café. A statue of the Venezuelan revolutionary leader, Simón Bolívar, has been added because his mother, María Concepción Palacio y Blanco, was born in the town. It was the first statue of the great liberator to be erected in Spain. On the southern side of the square is the palace of the counts of Gomera. Dominating the eastern side is the church of **Nuestra Señora de los Angeles** and the 16th-century former convent of Francis of Assisi, the latter now housing the **Casa de la Cultura**, where exhibitions are held, and a small natural history museum. On the northern side are the ochre walls of La Quinta Roja *(see page 131)*, a beautiful hotel with a bar and restaurant. It is also a centre of activities in the region, with information on walks and tours. Drop in to find out what is going on – and look out for the turtles in the garden.

Another smart hotel is the San Roque *(see page 131)*, in the Casa Noriega just to the west of the square, and its contemporary sculptures show the town's awareness of the arts as well as its heritage. A museum of contemporary art is housed in the 17th-century former convent of Santo Domingo. One other huge convent in the town is the 18th-century Franciscan convent, a closed order that still maintains around 15 nuns.

West of Garachico

The road heading west out of Garachico goes past the **Playa del Muelle** and up to a headland where the **Monumento a los Emigrantes Canarios** shows a figure with a suitcase and

Monument to the Emigrants

a hole in his heart setting off for a better life in America. There has been large scale emigration from this corner of the island, especially to Venezuela, and many towns and villages celebrate the day of Nuestra Señora del Buen Viaje, Our Lady of the Good Journey, on 31 August.

The nearest good beach to Garachico is a little further on, the **Playa La Caleta de Interián**.

As the road heads west, the countryside starts to flatten, smoothing a path first through sleepy **Los Silos** and arriving at **Buenavista del Norte**. Built around a central square with a small pavilion, its low, white houses have a languid, southern feel. The church of Nuestra Señora de los Remedios was refurbished after a serious fire in 1966.

The road leading from Buenavista continues all the way to **Faro del Teno**, the lighthouse at the island's northwestern tip where bird-watchers make for, on the lookout for ospreys, Barbary falcons and Cory's shear-waters. Road signs warn motorists of the dangers of landslides, which tend to occur mainly in windy and

Picturesque Masca

wet weather. La Gomera and La Palma are in view as you reach the headland, and at the lighthouse at **Punto del Teno** you can see down the entire west coast.

From Buenavista the road heads inland, past vines and signs for cheese for sale, and up through a changing mass of vegetation, with poppies lining the road. Among geolog-ical curiosities is the **Montañeta del Palmer**, which has been sliced like a cake for the extraction of *picón*, a gravel made of lava which is spread on agricultural land to retain moisture in the soil.

At the **Mirador del Baracán** there is a view down over both coasts. Bees hum as they potter about the aromatic plants, swifts dart overhead and there are walking paths off into the Teno Park.

Masca

The jewel of Tenerife's northwest is **Masca**, a cluster of buildings tipped over the side of the hill in a stunning setting above the sea. Approached over the hills from Buenavista or along the dramatic ribbon of road that flutters down from Santiago del Teide, Masca is not much more than a hamlet. It has approximately 100 inhabitants and it was off the tourist map until the road to it was eventually constructed in 1991.

Near the roadside, where cars squeeze into the few parking spaces, there are a couple of restaurants with terraces where you can have cactus ice cream with goat's yoghurt and honey, or suck cactus and papaya juice through a straw. Among the clutch of attractive buildings just below is a small museum of local finds.

The forest fires of July 2007, which burnt more than 15,000 hectares (37,000 acres) of land, engulfed the town, and charred remnants of a number of houses are a sad reminder of the event. Fortunately no lives were lost as the village was evacuated in time. The six-hour round hike into the narrow Barranco de Masca and down to the beach is now closed while the path is made safe after damage sustained in the fire, and a new metal bridge is being constructed to replace the wooden one that burned down.

El Tanque

El Tanque

The road above the coast at Garachico leads to **El Tanque**, a district of five hamlets scattered among pastureland in patchworks of fields between sweeping mountains. El Tanque is a small town overlooking the sea, centred on a corn exchange, the Casa de la Alhóndiga, that was once the town's meeting place. Mirador Lomo Molino is yet another great viewpoint on this route.

Continuing along this road, it is something of a surprise to see blue-robed 'bedouins' in camel trains. The **Camello Center** (Carretera General del Norte 4; tel: 922 13 61 91; open 1–5.30pm; <www.camellocenter.com>) offers donkeys as well as camels for hire on their half-hour excursions.

The road now climbs to reach the **Erjos** mountain pass (1,117m/3,664ft), where paths lead down to old farmhouses in the valleys. This pass divides north from south, and from here the full

Los Gigantes Harbour

southern heat brings only cacti and *malpaís* to the dry scrubland. It meets the road up from Masca at **Santiago del Teide**, a sunny white town in a broad valley. To the east is **Montaña del Chinyero**, the last volcano to erupt on the island, in 1909.

The village of **Arguayo**, situated just beyond, is famous for its ceramics, and the **Taller y Museo Alfarero Cha Domitila** (open Tues–Sat 10am–1pm, 4–7pm; free) is a museum and workshop showcasing traditional earthenware.

Los Gigantes to San Juan

Boats that sail to Masca bay are just part of the flotilla of pleasure craft berthed in **Los Gigantes**. This port, at the bottom of a steep hill, is the island's premier diving centre *(see page 85)* and the possibilities for water activities are endless. The port looks directly out at the *acantilado*, the cliff that rises sheer in front of it – this is the dramatic 800-m (2,625-ft) wall of the Teno massif, where the boat-less Guanche thought that the world came to an abrupt end. The cliff also drops fairly rapidly beneath the sea, making deep diving accessible.

The area's geography means that the only beach in Los Gigantes is tiny, but there is a good swimming pool, Piscina la Laguillo, just up from the port. There is a much larger beach, **Playa de Arena**, at its sister resort, **Puerto Santiago**, which is within easy striking distance. These are all well developed, modern resorts on steepish hills that lack the boisterous nightlife associated with the bigger resorts further to the south. The next resort of **Alcalá**, also based on a fishing port, has natural pools to swim in. **San Juan**, about 8km (5 miles) south of Los Gigantes, looks more like a working fishing port, with a friendly family beach around the harbour, though plans to build a fish packing factory beside it have met with opposition from the pro-tourist lobby. On Wednesday and Sunday mornings a food and craft market attracts visitors from around the region. There are also a couple of dive schools and some good fish restaurants.

Inland from San Juan is **Guía de Isora**, a rural community where potatoes and tomatoes grow. Its church has two Madonnas by José Luján Pérez.

Row the Atlantic

One of the world's toughest sporting events is the Atlantic Rowing Challenge, 5,000 km (3,000 miles) from Los Gigantes to Barbados. Boats 7.3m (24ft) long are rowed by two oarsmen. Chay Blythe started the race in 1997, 30 years after his three-month trans-Atlantic crossing with John Ridgeway.

Sunlounging in the south

THE SOUTH

Served by Reina Sofia airport, the south of the island is where it is hot, so this is where holidaymakers go, mainly to the resorts in the *municipios* of Adeje and Arona, in the merged touristopolis of Playa de las Américas and Los Cristianos. Hotels, apartments and villas continue to spread along the coast, bringing greenery to the *malpaís*, the badlands. Near the airport is the longest beach on the island, El Médano. All along the shore back towards Santa Cruz are rocky bays as well as small fishing ports such as Los Abrigos and Abona where fish is fresh on the menu. An upper road, from Granadilla de Abona to Güímar, where Thor Heyerdahl discovered mystic 'pyramids', passes through some small villages with views all down the coast. Some 15km (10 miles) before Santa Cruz the road drops to the coast around Candelaria, the most important pilgrimage town in the Canary Islands.

The Big Resorts

You have to know where you are going when you arrive in **Playa de las Américas**. Built out of nothing in the 1970s, it has no natural centre or heart, the roads are often not sign-posted and directions are generally given by the names of hotels. If you are driving and try to head for the seafront to get your bearings, you will be disappointed. Most of the seafront belongs to the four- and five-star hotels and often the closest you will get to it in a vehicle is their car parks.

On the seafront you can see the spectacular hotel fantasies that make up various people's ideas of heaven, from Canarian villages to Mexican *haciendas*, tarts' boudoirs and the glories of ancient Rome. Most ambitious is **Mare Nostrum** *(see page 134)*, a 'resort' of five-star hotels that look like something out of a Cecile B. de Mille epic. It includes the Pirámide de Arona, the Pax Romana congress centre with a restaurant where you can dine accompanied by opera or chamber music, and the Charlie Max Night Club. Mare Nostrum overlooks a small beach, the **Playa de Camisón**.

A larger beach, the **Playa de las Vistas**, lies between here and Los Cristianos but the main beaches of **Playas de Troya** and **Playa del Bobo** are to the north of the

The built-up southwest coast resorts, near Fañabe

Barranco del Rey. There is a tourist information point at this gully, which is near the rowdy **Veronicas** strip, hub of more than 100 discos and nightclubs. Technically the *barranco* marks the municipal boundary between Arona and Adeje. The coast north of here is the Costa Adeje, which drifts seamlessly into the giant hotels of **San Eugenio**, **Torviscas**, **Fañabe** and

Watch the whales at Aquapark

Playa del Duque. The small harbour of **Puerto Colón** in San Eugenio is the centre for water activities, dolphin- and whale-watching boats, and diving *(see page 85)*. Inland from the port is a large **Aquapark**, just one of myriad activities.

There are no limits to the possibilities for entertainment in and around Playa de las Américas *(see page 92 for details)*. And there are plenty of opportunities to spend your money. On Thursdays and Saturdays follow the crowds to the market held near Plaza del Duque at the north of the resort. The plaza itself is home to a new shopping centre, with upmarket boutiques as well as chain stores such as Mango.

La Caleta just to the north of Playa del Duque is the last resort to retain its identity. A meal in one of the seafood restaurants on the harbour here gives a taste of the real Tenerife.

Los Cristianos

The starting point of these resorts was the port of **Los Cristianos**, which lies on the south side of Playa de las Américas. They are separated by the volcanic cone of Montaña Chayofita, but it is otherwise hard to see the join, and you can walk from one to the other along a 7-km (4-mile), palm-lined promenade, dotted with pizzerias and souvenir shops. The port is still active, its ferries serving the neighbouring islands of El Hierro, La Palma and La Gomera. The south-facing **Playa los Cristianos** and **Playa de las Vistas** are sheltered and the sea is shallow and safe. Mar de Ons, a kiosk on Playa de Vistas, offers numerous sea excursions, including deep-sea fishing and a pirate boat cruise (<www.mardeons-tenerife.com>).

Los Cristianos has an authentic atmosphere, especially around its main pedestrian street, Avenida de Suecia, where there are inexpensive *pensións*, and above the Paseo Marítimo, where a row of restaurants and bars offer sea views. Events and exhibitions are staged in the **Centro Cultural** where the tourist office is situated. At the far end of the beach an open area is the site of a lively Sunday market.

The Municipal Towns

Inland, keeping a distant but watchful eye on their progeny, are the municipality's main towns, Adeje and Arona. **Adeje**, the former seat of the Guanche government, has never minded much how it made money. At the top of the town is the remains of the **Casa Fuerte**, the stronghold of Pedro, Count

La Gomera

Christopher Columbus's last port of call before he headed into the unknown in 1492 was the island of La Gomera, now just 30 minutes away from Los Cristianos on Fred Olsen's Australian-built *Benchijigua*. When you step ashore at San Sebastián you will find yourself in quite a different world. This quiet, underpopulated island is just 24km (15 miles) across, but you need to get away from the port to find its rural secrets. At its centre is the Parque Nacional de Garajonay, a UNESCO World Heritage Site, which you have to pass through to get to the lovely Valle de Gran Rey. For the sunniest beach, take a bus to Playa de Santiago.

of Gomera and one of the Genoese de Ponte family, who ruled the roost along this coast. He fell in with another rogue, the Elizabethan pirate John Hawkins, and together they conducted illegal trade with South America, as well as legitimately dealing in African slaves. Hawkins, who was later knighted for his role in defeating the Spanish Armada, was the first Englishman to become involved in the slave trade, in 1562. Wooden stocks in the Casa Fuerte are a reminder of the time. The town has a pleasant, if steep Rambla, lined with bars and cafés, that leads to the Iglesia Santa Ursula, with a Gobelins tapestry among its contents and an 18th-century chapel that was once part of a Franciscan convent.

In the port of La Gomera

Turn left at the top of the Rambla for the Casa Fuerte, and then up to Olivia, the café-restaurant at the entry point to the **Barranco del Infierno** (tel: 922 78 28 85; open daily 8.30am–1.30pm; visitors must reserve in advance), one of the most dramatic ravines on the island and the main reason that so many visitors come to the town. Stout shoes and at least 1 litre of water per person are needed for the round-trip walk up to the waterfall at the head of the *barranco*, which takes around three hours. There is a surprising amount of plant life along the way. If nothing else, this walk can give those staying at the main resorts a flavour of the island's true nature.

Montaña Roja near El Médano, visible from Reina Sofia airport

Along the South Coast

New developments continue around the southern tip of the island, at **Palm Mar** and the **Costa del Silencio**, which are entirely man-made communities. Between the two is **Las Galletas**, a thoroughly local little beach and port where fish are sold on the quayside every morning, including Sundays, bringing many *tinerfeños* in search of a good catch. The seafront is a pleasant stroll, with delicious Italian ice creams at Yo-Yo. At the Calibri restaurant you can eat fresh fish, *azul* or *blanca* (oily or white fish), by the kilo.

Perhaps the best place for fish restaurants is **Los Abrigos**, the next port along, where restaurants line the lane leading down to the port and hospitable women invite you in to dine. Restaurant Los Abrigos, right at the end, is bursting at weekend lunchtimes and its fish list is as long as your arm. Although these are pleasant little ports, neither is a real resort and accommodation is all but non-existent.

The longest beach in Tenerife stretches several kilometres around the **Montaña Roja**, a volcanic lump that punctuates the bleak acres of arid coast by the airport. Cars line the road but there are few amenities on the khaki-coloured sand, which stretches from the naturist beach of **La Tejita** to the small port of **El Médano**. Sunbathers should watch out for sunstroke in this blistering heat, but many of the people who come here are in search of good waves, for this is the haunt of serious windsurfers, and major championships have been held with the aid of the *alisios*, the steady northeast trade winds. There's just the one building that breaks the beachscape: the Playa Sur Tenerife *(see page 132)* has been catering to windsurfers for decades. El Médano, at the end of the beach, also has accommodation and restaurants.

Further along is **Poris de Abona**, a small community with a little beach.

Granadilla de Abona to Güímar

Just outside El Médano on the road up to Granadilla de Abona is the **Cueva del Hermano Pedro**, the cave where the shepherd boy Peter de Betancurt prayed as a child. Of Norman descent, Brother Peter was born on 19 March 1626, at Vilaflor. At 23 he left for the Americas where he became a missionary in Guatemala and did charitable work among the poor, for which he was canonised in 2002. The cave has now become a pilgrim site.

The old town of **Granadilla de Abona** is in the process of being spruced up.

Surfers off El Médano

A corner of Granadilla

It can seem deserted after the clamour of the coast. There is an attractive hotel here, the Hotel Rural Senderos de Abona *(see page 132)* in a mansion dating from 1856, with a restaurant, El Terrero, open in the evenings. Clock chimes emanate from the church opposite, dedicated to St Anthony of Padua. A number of the houses in the old town are being restored, especially in Calle Arquitecto Morrero, just down from the church, where one has become a *casa rural*. Next door is the small **Museo de la Historia de Granadilla de Abona** (open Mon–Fri 10am–2pm and 4–8pm, Sat 10am–1pm; free), a museum of local history. At the bottom of the street are derelict tobacco drying sheds; plans are afoot to turn them into a hotel and spa. There are several recommended walks in the mountains above Granadilla.

The upper road continues through sleepy old villages surrounded by terraced fields, many of them abandoned. At **Arico el Nuevo** there is also a sense of desertion, of pretty old buildings done up and awaiting some purpose.

The road dives in and out of a succession of deep gullies, the *barrancos*. Pigeons and doves of every colour appreciate the rocks for nesting, while the larger caves have been put to good use as storage space. At the **Mirador de Don Martín** there is a view over the Valle de Güímar where pineapple, avocado, banana, chirimoya, guava, cereal and vines are cultivated.

Ancient Temples

Some of the dry stone terraces here, known as *molleros* or *majones*, look like the bases of pyramids and it is no surprise to find the **Parque Etnográfico Pirámides de Güímar** (open daily 9.30m–6pm; admission fee; <www.piramidesdeguimar. net>) above the town of Güímar. This park is the work of an extraordinary man, Thor Heyerdahl, who lived in Tenerife from 1994 until his death in 2002. In that time he discovered what he believed to be the Guanches' cult of building flat-topped, step-sided pyramids for sun worship. The ship-owner and fellow Norwegian, Fred Olsen, bought land for the park and helped to develop it into a research centre.

Through Heyerdahl's expeditions on the balsa raft *Kon-Tiki* and the reed raft *Ra*, he made connections between the civilisations of Egypt and Mexico. Several acres of buildings have been uncovered. Replicas of his rafts are on show, and

Parque Etnográfico Pirámides de Güímar

the links between the indigenous peoples of North Africa, the Americas and the Pacific are speculated upon in a museum.

Güímar is a working town of 15,000, known for its wines and with a number of traditional, male-dominated *tascas (see page 101)*. It has two good churches, both with coffered *mudéjar* ceilings. The parish church at the top of the town has an exceptionally elaborate silver altarpiece, and the curiously arranged church of San Domingo, in the former monastery of the same name, is by the town hall in a shady square.

The tourist office is in the Casa de Artesana in Avenida de Obispo Perez Cácarez, the main shopping street, where you can find information on walks in the Malpaís de Güímar. This semi-desert wasteland surrounds the Montaña Grande below the town and spreads down to **Puertito de Güímar** on the coast. Here there is a pebble beach, and outside the town, in the direction of the Club Náutico, is a sandy shore.

Guanche chiefs, Candelaria

Candelaria

The name Candelaria, 'giver of light', means only one thing in the Canary Islands: a venerated Madonna, who is the islands' patron saint. The town of **Candelaria**, on the coast, is dominated by the 1950s basilica (open daily 7.30am–1pm and 3–7.30pm; free) that contains her image, and thousands of pilgrims gather in the square outside every August on the Feast of the Assumption, when the conversion of the Guanches to Christianity is re-enacted.

Lining the sea side of the square are statues by José Abad of the seven Guanche *menceys*, or chiefs, who were in power at the time of de Lugo's conquest. Six of them didn't have too much to be thankful for when Christianity arrived. One, however, the

Souvenir of the Candelaria Madonna

mencey of Güímar, was already half way to becoming a Christian without realising it. Inside the church the story of the discovery of the Madonna and her healing powers is told in delightful but murky paintings. They show the wooden Madonna holding Jesus in one hand and a candle in the other, arriving on the shore in 1392. Two shepherds discovered her, and one of them cut his hand on his knife while trying to ascertain if the statue was alive. The wound stopped bleeding the moment that he touched her. When news got out, the *mencey* of Güímar, who was the shepherd's leader, had a shrine built for the Madonna, and when the Spanish conquerors arrived, they convinced him that his conversion was underway. De Lugo was thus able to persuade him to join the Spaniards in their subjugation of the island's pagan Guanche tribes.

When visiting Candelaria, try to go on a Wednesday. From 10am to 3pm a large, bustling market covers the main square.

The tourist office, on the seafront, has information on the town as well as walks into the surrounding countryside. There is also an interesting ceramics workshop and museum (Centro de Alfarero de Candelaria, Calle Isla de la Gomera 7).

WHAT TO DO

Tenerife's highlights and attractions lie in its natural resources. With a pleasant climate and a diverse landscape of dramatic coasts and exotic interior, the island is ideal for all kinds of outdoor activities. Many visitors come here to walk in the hills and enjoy the abundant flora and search out unique fauna. Much of the island is given to parks and nature reserves. The sea, dropping steeply to the depths of the Atlantic, is a favourite for both experienced and novice divers, and there are whales and dolphins to watch if you don't want to get wet. In the larger towns and resorts many entertainments and activities are laid on for visitors, too, from theme parks and medieval spectaculars to folk concerts and Canary Island wrestling.

OUTDOOR ACTIVITIES

Walking and Hiking

The island is still crossed with the many paths that until comparatively recently were the only way of getting around the island. Today the Spanish Nature Conservation Institute ICONA has mapped *senderos turisticas* (tourist paths) and distributes free leaflets on walks in the Orotava Valley, the Anaga Hills and Teno Rural Park. More ambitious walkers, who have no coronary or respiratory concerns, will want to conquer the lavascapes of the *cañadas* around El Teide, and information can be found at the information centre for the Parque Nacional del Teide *(see page 52)*. Walking maps, guides and books, often available in English, can be found in most bookshops *(librerías)*. Cruz del

Windsurfer picking up the trade winds at El Médano

Carmen Mirador has information on walking in the Anaga Hills, where the Albergue Montes de Anaga *(see page 127)* makes a good base. Other hotels that make good bases for walking are La Quinta Roja in Garachico *(see page 131)* for the northwest and the Hotel de VillAlba in Vilafor for the southwest *(see page 134)*.

Patea Tus Montes (tel: 922 23 04 28, <www.pateatus montes.com>) offer hikes around the island guided by locals, as well as climbing and mountainbiking.

You can also plan walks before you go by checking out <www.tenerifenatural.com> or <www.webtenerife.com>.

Motorbikes can be hired for an exhilarating day trip

Bikes and Karting

Mountain bikes can be hired in main tourist centres, such as Mountainbike Active in Calle Mazaroco near the bus station in Puerto de la Cruz (tel: 922 37 60 81, <www. mtb-active.com>). Try Rafting Bike (tel: 699 94 46 22) if you don't fancy all that pedalling. Trips are downhill all the way, starting at 2,250 metres (7,400ft) and travelling 35km (22 miles) down to the sea.

Motorbikes can also be hired. Bikes range from 50cc scooters (€30 a day) to 650cc models at €85 a day.

Quad bikes can be ridden in Quad Park in Arona, opposite Aqualand, tel: 922 72

51 76. At Quad Safari, tel: 922 71 45 96; <www.tenerife-abc.com/quadbikesafari>, the excursions last either 90 minutes or three hours. The Quad Safari office is based in the Malibu Park centre in Playa de las Américas.

Jeep tours are available from Tamarán Alquiler Jeep Safari in Playa de las Américas, tel: 922 79 47 57, <www.tamaran.com>.

Tenerife's diverse flora include the pomegranate flower

Flora Spotting

The island flora is one of the reasons for visiting Tenerife. It brightens the island throughout the year. May and June, when the roadsides are overwhelmed with flowers, are the best months to come, but there is something to see all year round. Flora endemic to the island can be found in many different habitats. Cañada del Teide supports alpine plants such as the Teide echium ('The Pride of Tenerife'), while desert-like species are found around El Médano in the *malpaís* lands of the south. Some of these are very rare, and no fewer than 19 have been identified as now being under threat.

When the islands were used as a staging post between the New World and Spain, many South American species were introduced. Some can be seen at the Jardín de Aclimatación de la Orotava in Puerto de la Cruz, sometimes called simply the Jardín Botánico. The Jardín Tropical in Playa de las Américas also has a substantial collection.

The Museu de la Naturaleza y el Hombre in Santa Cruz gives an account of the island's flora and its bookshop has several books and charts on the subject.

Birdwatching

Birdwatchers should bring binoculars. The island is not abundant with birds, but there are some unusual ones that can be seen, particularly those unique to the island *(see page 10)*. Walking in the hills and forests of the national parks will be rewarding. Around the lighthouses on the three extreme points of the island (Faro de Teno, Faro de la Rasca and Faro de Anaga) you will find the best views of seabirds.

Look out for notices about organised local walks. Recommended books include: *A Birdwatcher's Guide to the Canary Islands* by Tony Clarke and David Collins, *Finding Birds in the Canary Islands* by Dave Gosney and *Where to Watch Birds in Tenerife* by Eduardo García del Rey.

Horse and Camel Riding

Stables offering hacks through the countryside include Centro Hípico los Brezos (tel: 922 56 72 22, <www.clubhipico losbrezos.com>) near Puerto de la Cruz, with three-hour rides over the Tacoronte Hills on weekdays only. El Rancho Grande near Amarilla Golf (tel: 922 730 319/687 90 55 11) caters for children and adults. Prices are around €20 an hour. Donkeys as well as camels can be hired at the Camello Center in El Tanque, in the northwest (tel: 922 13 61 91).

Hang-gliding

There is no shortage of high spots for hang-gliders to jump from. Courses are available, for beginners and the experienced at the Parapente Club del Sur, Edificio Esmeralda 39, Callao Salvaje, Adeje, tel: 922 78 13 57.

Golf

Spain's second oldest course, the Real Club de Golf de Tenerife (<www.realclubgolf tenerife.com>), is the island's oldest, opened in 1932. Near Los Rodeos airport, with good views, it looks rather like an English park, and has an exclusive air. Most of the other courses are around Playa de la Américas in the south. Golf Las Américas (<www.golf-tenerife.com>), just by the resort, opened in 1998 with the accompanying five-star GL Hotel Las Madrigueras. Golf del Sur (<www.golfdelsur.net>) in San Miguel de Abona has hosted a number of tournaments. Also located in San Miguel de Abona is the Amarilla Golf and Country Club (<www.amarillagolf.es>). Los Palos Golf Center (<www.golflospalos.com>) in Las Galletes, a nine-hole course, welcomes beginners. Green fees are around €30.

Kitesurfing is becoming popular

WATER ACTIVITIES

Just about every waterborne activity ever thought of is available on the west and south coasts of the island. Some, like whale-watching and scuba diving, allow you to experience the area's unique wildlife, whilst others, such as windsurfing, take advantage of the superb natural conditions.

Diving

The waters around the island swiftly drop to dramatic depths, with caves and caverns and a diversity of ocean life that have made Tenerife dive sites some of the most popular in the world. Sea temperatures are conducive year-round, from an average 20°C (68°F) in winter to 24°C (75°F) in summer. Tuna, barracuda, sting rays, eagle rays and morays are among the big fish; rainbow wrasse and trigger fish among the small delights. Sponges, anemones, and red and yellow gorgonias also lie in wait. Though the waters plunge to 2,000m (6,500ft), there is a legal depth of 40m (130ft) imposed on dives, many of which are multi-level. Operators offer courses from beginner to divemaster, with equipment and cameras available for hire, and video and film-making possibilities. Dive trials for beginners start at around €50 but note that Spanish law precludes under-16s from scuba diving. Most diving centres *(buceo)* operate on the west coast, with companies concentrated in Los Gigantes (Marina Los Gigantes Dive Center, tel: 922 86 80 95, <www.losgigantesmarina. com>), Playa San Juan, Los Cristianos and around the corner in Las Galletas (Buceo Tenerife Diving Center, tel: 922 73 10 15, <www.buceotenerife.com>).

Whale- and Dolphin-Watching

A number of vessels offer whale- and dolphin-watching trips. The Canaries are on one of the main whale migration routes: one third of all species pass through the islands each year.

Two glass-bottom catamarans, the *Tropical Delfin* and *Royal Delfin* (tel: 900 70 07 09, <www.tenerife-dolphins-whales.com>) operate out of Puerto Colón allowing you to see the animals underwater. The owners of the wooden sailing boat *Katrin*, based in Los Gigantes, conduct ethical dolphin-watching tours, mooring off Masca Bay, where you can

Seeing dolphins in the wild is an exhilarating experience

snorkel from the boat. *Nashira Uno* is a catamaran that runs three trips daily from Los Gigantes; the most common sightings are bottlenose dolphins and the long-finned pilot whale (tel: 922 861918).

Fishing

Shark, blue marlin, tuna and barracuda are the Big Game to be fished off the west coast. Boats can be hired in Los Gigantes (Punta Umbria V, tel: 922 86 19 18), Playa San Juan or Los Cristianos.

Windsurfing

All the windsurfers head for El Médano on the south coast, where the bay between the town and the Montaña Roja is one of the world's top 10 venues for the sport. The Playa Sur Tenerife Hotel, where you can hire boards, is one of the main places to hang out *(see page 132)*.

SPECTATOR SPORTS

Football

Club Deportivo Tenerife – known as the *blanquiazules* (the blue and whites) – is the island's main football team, playing at the Heliodoro Rodriguez Lopez Stadium in Santa Cruz. The team plays in the second division of La Liga. Games are generally on Sunday afternoons.

Canary Wrestling

Lucha Canaria is a popular island sport which takes place in village halls and special *terreros* all round the country. It is played on a league basis, in which teams of 12 wrestlers fight individual bouts *(bregas)* in sand rings 10m (33ft) in diameter. The object is to force any part of your opponent's body to the floor using whatever means you can. Exhibition

Acrobatics at Loro Parque

bouts are often staged as part of local fiestas when *juego de palo* or *banot,* a traditional stick-fight, is frequently also put on.

FOR CHILDREN

The island's beaches are a great place for children to while away many an hour, though there is no perceptible tide and the land disap-

Science and Cosmos Museum

pears into the depths very quickly. This means that there is little sea life in the rockpools and on the beaches.

The resorts are well supplied with play parks, rides, zoos and gardens. **Loro Parque** is a big day out, with killer whale, dolphin, sea-lion shows, an aquarium, a cinema and a large collection of parrots. Transport is provided from Puerto de la Cruz. **Aqualand** in Costa Adeje is a waterpark with swimming pools, water slides and a dolphinarium. Free transport is provided from both Playa de las Americas and Los Cristianos. Primates star in **Tenerife Zoo** and eagles soar in **Parque Las Aguilas**; both attractions are near Los Cristianos. There is a botanic garden and zoo, with camel rides, at **Oasis del Valle** in La Orotava. In Valle de Orotava, **Pueblochico** is a model village of outdoor doll's-house sized Canarian buildings with botanic gardens and dragon trees in miniature. The **Museo de la Ciencia y el Cosmos** *(see page 36)* in La Laguna is a hands-on museum with lots of interest for children, as is the **Museu de la Naturaleza y el Hombre** in Santa Cruz *(see page 29)*. **Casa de los Cáceres** is a doll and teddy bear museum in Icod de los Vinos near the famous dragon tree.

SHOPPING

Many **designer shops** have outlets in the big resorts, but there is home-grown talent, too. Spain is known for its well-made and inexpensive **leather goods**, from bags and belts to jackets and coats. Shoes in particular are relatively inexpensive and well designed.

Embroidery and **lace-making** are traditional island crafts. Tablecloths and cushion covers with detailed patterns are a speciality. It is best to buy from a shop, such as the Casa de los Balcones in La Orotava, or one of its 11 branches, rather than from a street seller, whose goods are often made in Taiwan.

Island **craft** speciality shops include Artenerife, <www.artenerife.com>, which has several outlets across the island, including one in Casa de la Aduana in Puerto de la Cruz and one in Casa Torrehermosa in La Orotava. Lava rock and obsidian is used in **sculptures** and a variety of **ceramics** are on sale. Pots are generally plain earthenware, many made in Guanche fashion. There are also copies of their fertility goddesses and die-stamps. At Los Calados Artesanía in La Laguna you can buy Canarian costumes.

Silver jewellery is worth looking at and **pearl** shops are a speciality. Tenerife Pearl has half a dozen outlets and a main building with an exhibition at Armeñime on the main road between Adeje and Los Gigantes.

Cigars, hand-rolled from local tobacco, are a good buy. Souvenirs include giant ones

At the market

Bargaining is expected in the flea markets and at street-side stalls run by the North African merchants, but beware of 'special offers' from these traders, whose goods may include ivory jewellery or leather or fur goods from endangered species. Not only will you be supporting the killing of rare animals, but import of such items into Europe and the US is subject to heavy penalties.

50cm long. Fancy cigarettes are also available, in pastel colours and prettily boxed. Volcanic gravel impregnated with perfume is a novelty – roll the cigar in it before smoking to sweeten the aroma of the fumes.

Local **wines**, hard to find abroad (or at the airport), make good souvenirs. Try to buy from the Casa del Vino La Baranda at El Sauzal. Tenerife **honey** *(miel)* comes in various guises; there are hand-made signs for it along the roadside. The best is from Las Cañadas del Teide – from bees that suck the nectar of Teide broom. Find out all about the different kinds in

Straw hats

the Casa de la Miel by the Casa del Vino in El Sauzel. Other groceries to bring home might include jars of red or green *mojo (see page 97), bienmesabe (see page 98)* or cactus, papaya and other exotic preserves. Current restrictions ban the transport of any liquid over 100ml in your hand luggage, so be sure to pack any purchases in your suitcase for the hold.

NIGHTLIFE

Much of Tenerife's nightlife takes place on the streets. There are often spontaneous gatherings in the squares and on the beaches, and music spills out onto the pavements from bars. Holidaymakers can join in the general mood of relaxation.

In tourist hotspots there are plenty of nightclubs and discos, as well as concerts, and little starts before midnight. As might be expected, **Playa de las Américas** has the most lavish nightlife on the island. Veronica's is the best known strip, with around 100 bars and discos that keep going until dawn. Some of the most extravagant shows are at Pirámide de Arona, Avenida de las Américas (tel: 922 75 75 49). Tropicana (tel: 902 33 12 34) stages 'Cuban' song-and-dance spectaculars. The Castillo San Miguel (tel: 922 70 02 76, <www.castillosanmiguel.com>), signposted off the *autopista sur* at San Miguel, has medieval nights.

In **Puerto de la Cruz**, Azúcar (Calle Iriarte 1) is set in a period house and doesn't look like a nightclub from outside, but inside buzzes with latin beats and locals showing off their salsa skills. Café de Paris at Avenida de Colón is a restaurant with dancing that attracts a slightly older crowd. In **Santa Cruz**, Lounge Gabanna (Avenida de la Constitución) is one of the hottest nightspots in town. **La Laguna** has a busy and varied nightlife scene thanks to its large student population.

The **Auditorio de Tenerife** in Santa Cruz is the home of the admired Orchestra Sinfonica de Tenerife, whose concerts run from the beginning of September until the end of July. It is also the main venue for the island's opera and dance.

Where to Gamble

- Puerto de la Cruz: Casino Taoro (tel: 922 38 05 50) is probably one of the best casinos in Europe. Another casino has recently opened in Lago Martiánez (tel: 922 38 59 55) on the seafront.
- Santa Cruz: The Casino Santa Cruz is beside the Hotel Mencey.
- Playa de las Américas: There is a casino in the ground floor of the Hotel Gran Tinerife (tel: 922 79 37 58), with machines and tables.

  You will need your passport for entry to the casinos.

The Santa Cruz Carnaval is one of the most lavish in Europe

FESTIVALS

Fiestas are a part of island life, and there is a fair chance of seeing one during any stay – 30 days are officially set aside for festivals, based on the church calendar *(see page 95)*.

Carnaval

Undoubtedly the most spectacular festival is the pre-Lent carnival. Puerto de la Cruz and Santa Cruz are both overtaken by the event, which is said to rival Rio. Fired by a Latin American fervour, it requires the same great lengths of preparation. Events last for nearly two weeks, starting with the election of a Carnival Queen and climaxing on Shrove Tuesday with the *coso*, the grand parade, with floats on various themes, and everyone in the fanciest carnival dress. There is a strong transvestite element and dancers are accompanied by *murgas*, groups singing satirical songs. The event draws to a close on

Ash Wednesday with El Entierro de la Sardina (the burial of the sardine), a mock funeral attended by people in outrageous outfits, who beat their breasts and shed crocodile tears.

Corpus Christi

One of the most widely celebrated religous festivals on the island is the eight days (Octavo) of Corpus Christi at the end of May or the beginning of June. The best places to see it celebrated are La Laguna and La Orotava, where pavements are covered with spectacular carpets made out of flowers and a wide array of colours from volcanic sand. The procession that makes its way over them crushes the flower petals and fills the air with their scent.

Romerías

Corpus Christi marks the beginning of the Romería season of local festivals involving food, wine and dancing. Again it is La Orotava and La Laguna that put on the biggest shows, with, respectively, the Romería de San Isidro in mid-June and the Romería de San Benita a fortnight later. Arico, Granadilla, Güímar and Icod also have large Romerías during the month.

Local fiesta, local dress

Assumption

The biggest pilgrimage takes place on the day of the Assumption (15 August) at Candelaria, where the statue of Our Lady of Candelaria, patron saint of the Canary Islands, is paraded in the streets. On the day before there is a re-enactment of the appearance of the Virgin to the Guanche shepherds.

Festivals

For public holidays, see page 116.

January: *Cabalgata de los Reyes* (Procession of the Three Kings, Santa Cruz and Garachico), with costumes, brass bands, camel cavalcades.

February/March: *Carnaval*, Santa Cruz's extravaganza; also in Puerto de la Cruz.

March/April: *Semana Santa* (Holy Week): solemn pre-Easter processions in many towns and cities throughout the island.

April: local fiestas on 25th (Icod, Tegueste).

May: spring festivals, opera festival (Santa Cruz). *Fiestas de la Cruz* (all places with Cruz [cross] in their name): processions, festivities and fireworks. San Isidro (Los Realejos), San Isidro (Santa María de la Cabeza, with large firework display).
Fiesta de Corpus Christi (late May or early June, La Laguna, La Orotava and elsewhere); beautiful flower carpets.

June: *Romería de San Isidro* (La Orotava), *Romería de San Benito* (La Laguna); ox-drawn carts laden with local produce. Local fiestas (Arico, El Sauzal, Grandill, Güímar, Icod).

July: *Fiesta del Mar* (Festival of the Sea, Los Realojos, Puerto de la Cruz, Santa Cruz). *Fiesta de la Virgen del Carmen*, patron saint of seamen. *Romerías de Santiago Apóstol* (Festival of St James, Santa Cruz): pilgrimage, fireworks. Local fiestas (Candelaria, La Laguna, Los Realojos, Santiago del Teide).

August: *Fiesta de la Asunción* (Assumption, Candelaria): re-enactment of the appearance of the Blessed Virgin to the Guanches. Local fiestas (Garachico, Los Cristianos).

September: *Fiestas del Santísimo Cristo* (La Laguna, Tacaronte): floats, fireworks, sports, theatre and poetry. Local festivals (Güímar, Guía de Isora). Grape harvest.

October: Local fiesta (Granadilla).

November: *Todos los Santos* (All Saints Day). *San Andrés* (St Andrew's): new wine tasting festival in Icod, La Orotava and Puerto de la Cruz.

December: *Navidad* (Christmas). *Noche Vieja* (New Year's Eve).

EATING OUT

There is no shortage of restaurants serving chicken and pizza in the resorts, and Chinese restaurants are a popular alternative for *tinerfeños*. But any visitor should concentrate on getting to know the local dishes, which are the staple of most restaurants across the island. These are based on home-grown pulses and vegetables, fish from the Atlantic, and meat from indigenous animals. Portions are generally healthy, and establishments are usually relaxed, so you can be as picky as you like. *Cocina Canario*, *cocina casa linga* and *típico* are signs of local cooking. *Tapas*, small dishes to eat as appetisers, are served in many bars and restaurants and they can be made into a meal. And there are eminently palatable wines from the island's five recognised denominated regions.

Spices on sale at market

WHAT TO EAT

Vegetables

One of the mainstays of the island are potatoes, and the fact that they are called *papas* here, as they are in South America, and not *patatas*, as they are in Spain, is a clue to their affinities. There are no blights known to the local tuber, and there are a dozen regularly grown

Papas, the island's speciality

Andean varieties, notably *papa negra*, black potatoes. The size of squash balls and the colour of wood ash, they are usually prepared *arrugadas* or 'wrinkled', boiled in their jackets in highly salted water (traditionally sea water) and usually served with a *mojo* sauce.

Mojo sauces, to accompany both fish and meat dishes, are made of olive oil, herbs and spices and come in two colours – red and green. These are either poured on to a dish or served in their own bowls for you to dip into or spoon out. Restaurants have their own recipes. The red *mojo picón* has dried peppers, chilli or paprika; the green *mojo verde* is made of parsley or, more distinctly, coriander *(cilantro)*.

Sweet potatoes, or yams, are also grown and can be seen piled high in the markets, but they are by and large absent from restaurant menus.

Another Latin American influence is corn cobs *(piñas de millo)*, used widely in soups and stews including *puchero canario*, the traditional stew of the Canaries, in which a variety of local vegetables is likely to appear, such as chickpeas *(gabanzos)*, kidney beans and *bubango*, a particular kind of marrow.

Fried fish

Soups are plentiful and include *vieja ropa* ('old clothes'), a kind of *minestrone* into which anything goes, and *rancho canario*, a watercress soup.

Salad ingredients are generally fresh, as you might expect, and tomatoes are particularly tasty.

Gofio

If you eat anywhere on the island, it won't be long before you encounter *gofio*, the staple food of the Guanche. This is toasted ground corn, generally maize, but sometimes barley or wheat or even chickpeas, and it is served in a variety of ways. It can be added to soups as a thickener, and it comes as a seasoned broth, *escaldon*, usually served in an earthenware dish. It is also used as an accompaniment to dishes, or as a dessert, when it is made into a milk pudding *(frangollo)* or a mousse *(mus)* served with *bienmesabe* ('it tastes good to me') made from almonds and honey.

Meat

Tenerife is not a great meat-eating land. There is beef and pork, but the principal interest lies in local goat *(cabrito)*, usually simply grilled, and rabbit *(conejo)*. *Conejo en salmorejo* is a stew of diced rabbit in a marinade, which is fried and boiled in its own juices and may be served with *papas arrugadas. Costillas con papas de piñas de millo* is a stew of pork ribs, potatoes and corn cobs.

Fish

Fish is the glory of the island. The deep cold surrounding waters produce meaty flesh with a lot of flavour. Even sardines, simply grilled, are delicious. Most visitors will have difficulty identifying many of these mid-Atlantic species, some of which do not exist in translation *(see below)*. Parrot fish *(vieja)* has such delicate scales that they are not cleaned for cooking, and you have to skim them off on your plate, moving the knife up from the tail. In fresh fish restaurants larger fish is often sold by the kilo, in which case you will find that white fish *(blanco)* is slightly more expensive

Fish on the Menu

Many of the exotic Atlantic fish you will see on the extensive menus in Tenerife are unlike any you will see in most of Spain, and some are not easily translated. These include:

Abadejo – pollack; *aguja azul* – blue marlin; *bacalao* – cod; *chipirón* – baby squid; *caballa* – horse mackerel; *cabrilla* – grouper; *cherne* – sea bass; *choco* – cuttlefish; *congrio* – conger eel; *burro* – donkey fish; *corvino* – corb; *dorado* – gilthead bream; *lenguado* – sole; *merluza* – hake; *mero* – grouper; *morena* – moray eel; *pez espada* – sword fish; *rodaballo* – turbot; *salema* – gold-lined bream; *salmoneta* – red mullet; *same* – gold bream; *sarda* – mackerel; *sargo* – white bream; *vieja* – parrot fish.

Delicious fresh fruit

than oily fish *(azul)*. There are local mussels *(lapas)*, and the large prawns *(gambas)* make an excellent *tapa*.

A *cazuelo* (stew) of fish is a good way to sample what is available. This is made with a wide variety of fish in recognisable chunks, with some vegetables added. Portions are generous.

Fruit

The island's exotic fruits arrive on the table whole or in juice drinks. Bananas are mostly of the small Dwarf Cavendish variety, and are sometimes served for breakfast with fried eggs and rice – a Cuban speciality. Interesting fruit to try includes prickly pear, *chirimoya* or custard apples and *níspero*, small yellow medlars that ripen in May. Roadside stalls are one way to find them fresh.

Papaya, mango and prickly pear (cactus) are all in abundance and are turned into fruit juices.

Cheese

There are a number of local cheeses to try out, made from both goats' and sheep's milk and varying in strength from mild to tangy. Cheese is not universally available and if you see any advertised on your travels around the island, it is well worth seeking out. Arico, in the island's south, is a cheese-making centre.

WHERE TO EAT

Good restaurants are to be found along the main roads, as well as in the main towns. *¡Que Bueno!*, a book of top restaurants, is published every year, with text in both Spanish and English, though its entries tend to be skewed towards the swankpots of the Costa Adeje.

Tascas and Bodegas

Tenerife has a tradition of *tascas*, small eating houses where you can also go just for a drink. A number of these have become rather smart in Santa Cruz and elsewhere, with cutting-edge young chefs trying to make their mark. At the same time they are cosy places to eat. *Bodegas*, *bodegones* and *bodeguitas*, originally wine houses, are fairly indistinguishable bars with *tapas* and even full meals provided. Pick what you want from a menu: there is no formality about having to have courses in any particular order, or with any particular accompaniment.

    Tinerfeños eat lunch, their main meal, around 2 or 3 pm, and dinner from around 9pm. A number of restaurants close on Sunday night and one day a week, often Monday.

WHAT TO DRINK

Tea and Coffee

There are plenty of places to drop in for a drink. Coffee is the leisure daytime drink of the island. As on mainland Spain, you can have *café solo* (equivalent of an espresso), *cortado* in a glass tumbler

Sign for fresh meats

with a little milk, *café con leche* with milk and *Americano* or *largo*, a solo with extra water. Occasionally you may be asked if you want a black *(negro)* or brown *(marrón)* roast. Cafés often do deals for breakfasts, including juice and perhaps a roll or croissant. Cakes and pastries are usually on offer, but away from the main towns fresh bread is not always available until later in the day, and a doughnut or a half-frozen croissant may be all there is.

Tea is generally a bag in hot water, but La Folie café, a wonderfully atmospheric little nightspot in Calle Santo Domingo, La Laguna, has pots of speciality teas.

Fresh orange and other juices are usually available and the local beer, Dorada, is a blond lager that will quench any thirst. Some of the more traditional bars don't have signs outside and you only know they are there when they are open.

Wine

Tenerife is the main wine-making Canary Island. Although it produces around 5 million litres a year, there is no guarantee that a local label will be on your restaurant wine list, but if it is there, you should choose it. House wines are often Riojas, which may be heavier than you want.

The island is divided into five *Denominaciónes de Origen* (DO), and because of the great difference in altitude, the grape harvest is staggered. If you are here on 29 November, the eve of St Andrew's day, make for the wine-tasting festivals in La Orotava, Puerto de la Cruz and, most entertainingly, Icod de los Vinos, where people slide on boards down the cobbled streets and make a racket with tin cans, echoing the barrel runs down to the former port.

Local spirits

Local rum *(ron)* is made from cane sugar. Sweet liqueurs include *ronmiel*, made from palm sap, and *cobana*, made from bananas.

The **Abona** DO region in the south reaches right up to Vilaflor which must make the vineyards about the highest in the world. They produce mainly white wines from a dozen grape varieties, plus a few reds and rosés.

Valle de la Orotava covers the municipalities of La Orotava, Realejos and Puerto de la Cruz, and produces full reds and whites.

Tacoronte-Acentejo is the best known and most productive of the regions, making young reds from Listán Negro and Negromoll grapes. Brands include Viña Norte, which has 600 growers and has been winning

Casa del Vino, El Sauzal

prizes since the 1990s, and Humboldt Tinto, which won a gold medal at the Vinalies Internationales in Paris in 2003.

Ycoden-Daute-Isora has a long history of producing light, aromatic reds as well as whites.

Valle de Güímar produces white wines from white grapes, including the Gual and Verdella, grown between 600 and 800m (2,000–2,600ft).

There is also a substantial amount of fortified wine made from Malvasía or muscatel grapes. Wineries *(bodegas)* are generally places where you can just drop in, and if you book ahead, some will show you around. The best place to find out about the island's wines is the Casa del Vino La Baranda *(see page 48)*. Or visit <www.bodegasinsularestenerife.es>.

To Help You Order

Could we have a table?	**¿Nos puede dar una mesa, por favor?**
Do you have a set menu?	**¿Tiene un menú del día?**
I would like...	**Quisiera…**
The bill, please	**La cuenta, por favor**

Deciphering the Menu

agua minerale	mineral water	**flan**	caramel custard
à la plancha	grilled	**helado**	ice cream
al ajillo	in garlic	**jamón serrano**	cured ham
al punto	medium	**judías**	beans
arroz	rice	**langosta**	lobster
asado	roast	**leche**	milk
atún	tuna	**mariscos**	shellfish
azúcar	sugar	**mejillones**	mussels
bacalao	cod	**morcilla**	black pudding
bocadillo	sandwich	**pan**	bread
boquerones	anchovies	**pescado**	fish
buen hecho	well done	**picante**	spicy
buey/res	beef	**poco hecho**	rare
café	coffee	**pollo**	chicken
calamares	squid	**postre**	dessert
callos	tripe	**puerco**	pork
cangrejo	crab	**pulpitos**	baby octopus
cerdo	pork	**queso**	cheese
cerveza	beer	**sal**	salt
champiñones	mushrooms	**ternera**	veal
chorizo	spicy sausage	**tortilla**	omelette
cocido	stew	**trucha**	trout
cordero	lamb	**salsa**	sauce
ensalada	salad	**vino**	wine
entremeses	hors-d'oeuvre	**verduras**	vegetables

HANDY TRAVEL TIPS

An A–Z Summary of Practical Information

A

ACCOMMODATION

Don't expect to find accommodation in every town or village; most hotels and apartments are centred on the main towns and resorts. But the island is not large and it is easy enough to make a base from which to explore. The standard of accommodation is generally high, and you are unlikely to have anything to complain about. Prices are reasonable and establishments are graded by a system that allows for many categories of accommodation and variations within each category. A hotel may be rated from one-star to five-star Gran Lujo (GL) which signifies top-of-the-range quality, but stars are not always directly reflected in the price. Most of the four- and five-star hotels are in the major southern resorts, and many offer deals. Santa Cruz de Tenerife and Puerto de la Cruz have a selection of lower-rated places. By law, prices must be displayed in hotel reception areas and in the rooms. Breakfast is not always included in the basic rate.

In addition to hotels there are plenty of apartments, which are graded with one to three 'keys', shown with symbols, depending on their amenities. There are also 'aparthotels', often graded as hotels, where each room or suite of rooms has its own kitchen facilities yet retains all the trappings of a hotel.

Package holidays tend to provide accommodation in hotel complexes and self-catering apartments. Private apartments, of which there are a large number on Tenerife, are advertised in local papers by individuals and agents.

a single/double room with bath/shower	**una habitación individual/doble con baño/ducha**
What's the rate per night?	**¿Cuál es el precio por noche?**
Is breakfast included?	**¿Está incluído el desayuno?**

There are also an increasing number of country houses and hotels (*casas rurales* and *hoteles rurales*), usually in traditional houses or *fincas* (country estates). The tourist offices have details, or visit <www.ecoturismocanarias.com>.

If you plan to arrive during the high season (late November to February, July and August), book accommodation well in advance through a travel agent or directly with the hotel. *(For accommodation suggestions, see page 127.)* For a full listing of accommodation consult the Spanish National Tourist Office *(see page 124)*, or local tourist offices.

AIRPORTS *(aeropuertos)*

There are two airports on the island. Most international flights use Reina Sofía Airport (Tenerife Sur) in the south (tel: 922 75 90 00). This is busiest on Tuesdays and Fridays. Buses run to Los Cristianos and Playa de las Américas (about 25 minutes) and to Puerto de la Cruz, (1hr 40 min). Los Rodeos Airport (Tenerife Norte) near La Laguna (tel: 922 63 59 98/63 58 00) handles inter-island air traffic as well as a few international flights. For general airport information, see <www.aena.es>.

B

BUDGETING FOR YOUR TRIP

To give you an idea of what to expect, here's a list of some average prices in euros. A euro is worth approximately £0.70 and approximately US$1.40.

Accommodation: Rates for a double room can range from as low as €25–30 at a *pensión* or *hostal* to as much as €360–420 at a top-of-the-range five-star hotel. A pleasant three-star hotel will cost in the range of €80. However, rates increase during the high season, beginning around late November and culminating with the Carnaval in February/March.

Apartments: Per night for a family apartment prices range from under €30 for one key to more than €75 for three keys. Discounts are often available for bookings of a week or more.

Attractions: Most museums and gardens charge a minimal entry fee of around €3. More expensive (€10–30) are the larger attractions such as the Pyramides de Güímar and theme parks such as Loro Parque.

Car hire: Around €35 a day.

Meals and drinks: In a bar, a continental breakfast (fresh orange juice, coffee and toast) will cost around €4. The cheapest three-course meal, *menú del día*, with one drink, in a small bar/restaurant, will be around €7. Dinner in a medium level restaurant will be about €20 per person, including wine. At the top restaurants expect to pay at least twice that amount.

Petrol: Around €0.65 a litre.

Sports: Golf green fees (per day) range from €45–55. Tennis court fees start at about €6 an hour. Horse riding starts at about €15 an hour.

Taxis: State regulated and inexpensive, a taxi journey within a town is unlikely to cost more than €3 or €4. The fare from Playa de las Américas to Reina Sofia airport is around €20–25.

| Do you accept travellers' cheques? | ¡Acepta usted cheques de viajero? |
| Can I pay with this credit card? | ¡Puedo pagar con esta tarjeta de crédito? |

C

CAMPING

Camping is not a common option on the island, and it is prohibited in the national parks. There is a site on the south coast, Camping Nauta Cañada Blanca, in Las Galletas (tel: 922 78 51 18; fax: 922 79 50 16).

CAR HIRE *(coches de alquiler) (See also DRIVING)*

Normally you must be over 21, sometimes 24, to rent a car, and you will need your passport, a major credit card and a valid driving licence that you have held for at least 12 months. Cars are generally manual transmission, and you will have to hunt around if you want an automatic vehicle.

There are around 100 local car-hire companies – 25 in Santa Cruz alone – and these tend to be cheaper than the better known companies. If you hire a car before you leave home, especially via the Internet, it is also usually cheaper. Local companies include Amigoauto <www.amigoautos.es>, and Tenerife Rent a Car <www.trc-cars.com>. All the big international companies (Avis, Europcar, Hertz) have offices at the airports and in the major towns. Hotels can recommend local firms.

I'd like to rent a car. for one day/week. Please include full insurance.	**Quisiera alquilar un coche. por un día/una semana. Haga el favor de incluir el seguro a todo riesgo.**

CLIMATE

With a temperature of a fairly steady 22°C (72°F) year-round, sunshine is the rule, but the weather in the north and eastern parts of the island can be changeable. In spring there is a cold and wet gust from the northwest, and in autumn the famous hot sirocco raises temperatures. Remember that the island is on a parallel with West Africa, and the temperatures in the southern resorts and in the *malpaís* can be high, so be careful not to burn. Up in the hills, it becomes much cooler, even in the town of La Laguna, and the trade winds keep the northeast of the island damp for most of the year. Temperatures drop to minus figures around El Teide's snowcapped summit and in the Cañadas.

CLOTHING

In addition to summer clothes and beachwear, don't forget a sweater or jacket for evenings. For excursions to high altitudes, you will also need warmer clothing and some sturdy shoes. Some protection from the rain may well come in handy.

Casual wear is the norm, although in five-star hotels, the best restaurants and the casinos, a jacket and tie, though not obligatory, will not be out of place for men.

Topless bathing is quite common, and is acceptable at most hotel pools. Beachwear, shorts, bikini tops and mini-skirts should not be worn when visiting religious places.

COMPLAINTS

By law, all hotels and restaurants must have official complaint forms *(hoja de reclamaciones)* and produce them on demand. The original of this triplicate document should be sent to the Ministry of Tourism; one copy remains with the establishment involved and one copy is given to you. Try to resolve your problem before going through this procedure, as it will be difficult for you to succeed in any claims once you have left the island. However, the very action of asking for the *hoja* may resolve the problem in itself, as tourism authorities take a serious view of malpractice, and can revoke or suspend licences.

You should also inform the local tourist office, or in serious cases the local police, of any complaints and seek their assistance.

CRIME

Theft is only really likely in tourist areas. Never leave anything of value in your car. Use the safe deposit box in your room for all valuables, including your passport. Burglaries of holiday apartments do occur, too, so keep doors and windows locked when you are absent. There is some opportunistic bag snatching and pocket picking in busy places such as markets or at fiestas. But Tenerife does not have a high crime rate. You must report all thefts to the local police within 24 hours for your own insurance purposes.

| I want to report a theft. | **Quiero denunciar un robo.** |

CUSTOMS AND ENTRY REQUIREMENTS

Most visitors, including citizens of all EU countries, the USA, Canada, Australia and New Zealand, require only a valid passport to enter Spain. Although Spain is in the EU, there is still a restriction on duty-free allowances at customs *(aduana)* when returning to the UK from the Canary Islands. This is: 200 cigarettes or 50 cigars or 250g smoking tobacco; 1 litre spirits over 22 percent or 2 litres under 22 percent, 2 litres of wine and £145 worth of goods.

D

DRIVING

Driving conditions. Drive on the right, pass on the left, yield right-of-way to all vehicles coming from your right.

Speed limits on the island are 120 km/h (74mph) on motorways, 100km/h (62mph) on dual highways, 90km/h (52mph) on country roads, 50km/h (31mph) in built-up areas and 20km/h (13mph) in residential areas.

Motorways are toll-free. In the main towns, and even in smaller provincial ones, traffic can be heavy and one-way systems confusing, especially as road signs are woefully inadequate.

Parking. You are more likely to find a parking space during lunch hours (2–4pm). Consider parking at the edge of towns and taking buses or taxis to the centre.

Many roads are narrow and twisting. Always slow down when passing through villages. At any time you may come across a herd of goats, a donkey and cart, a large pothole, or falling rocks.

Petrol. Petrol stations on main roads are often open 24 hours and most take credit cards. They are less frequent off the beaten track and often close at night and on Sundays. Most hire cars take unleaded petrol, which in Spain is called *sin plomo*.

Traffic police. Civil guards *(Guardia Civil)* patrol the roads on black motorbikes. In towns the municipal police handle traffic control. If you are fined for a traffic offence, you will have to pay on the spot.

Rules and regulations. Always carry your driving licence with you. It is also a good idea to have a photocopy of the important pages of your passport with you.

Seat belts are compulsory. Children under 10 must travel in the rear.

Road signs. Apart from the standard international pictographs you may encounter the following:

Aparcamiento	Parking
Desviación	Detour
Obras	Road works
Peatones	Pedestrians
Peligro	Danger
Salida de camione	Truck exit
Senso unico	One way

¿Se puede aparcar aqui?	Can I park here?
Llénelo, por favor, con super.	Fill the tank please, top grade.
Ha habido un accidente.	There has been an accident.

E

ELECTRICITY *(corriente eléctrica)*

The standard supply is 220v with continental-style two-pin sockets. North American 110v appliances will need a transformer.

EMBASSIES AND CONSULATES *(consulados)*

Santa Cruz de Tenerife: **United Kingdom**: Plaza Weyler, 8, 1st Floor, tel: 922 28 68 63, fax: 922 28 99 03; open Mon–Fri 9am–2pm. **Republic of Ireland**: Calle Castillo, 8, Fourth Floor A, tel: 922 24 56 71, fax: 922 24 99 57; open Mon–Fri 9am–1pm.

The nearest **US** consulate is in Las Palmas, capital of the neighbouring Gran Canaria island, at Edificio Arca, Calle Los Martinez de Escobar 3, Oficina 7, tel: 928 27 12 59, fax: 928 22 58 63. It opens 10am–1pm weekdays. For other countries' representations, you may have to call Madrid.

If you lose your passport, or run into trouble with the authorities or the police, contact your consulate for advice. Consulates can issue temporary passports for a fee. You will need a statement of loss or theft from the police, plus two passport size photographs.

Where is the American/ British consulate?	¿Dónde está el consulado americano/británico?

EMERGENCIES *(urgencia)*

The general emergency number is **112**. For the Civil Guard dial 062, for the local police dial 092 and for the national police dial 091.

Police	Policía
Fire	Fuego
Help!	¡Socorro!
Stop!	¡Deténgase!

There are the following hospitals in Tenerife:
Santa Cruz: Hospital Universitario de Canarias (tel: 922 67 80 00), Hospital Nuestra Senora de la Candelaria (tel: 922 60 20 00), Hospiten Rambla (tel: 922 29 16 00).

Playa de las Americas: Hospital Costa Adeje (tel: 922 75 26 26), Hospiten Sur (tel: 922 75 00 22).

Puerto de la Cruz: Hospiten Bellevue (tel: 922 38 35 51), Hospiten Tamaragua (tel: 922 38 05 12).

G

GAY AND LESBIAN TRAVELLERS

Major resorts in the Canary Islands have developed facilities for gay and lesbian travellers, including dedicated hotels. Check the website <www.gayinspain.com>.

GETTING TO TENERIFE

By air: There are many scheduled and cheap flights from all UK airports to Tenerife. The flight time is 3½–4½ hours, and the cost around £150–350. Check the web and the travel sections of weekend newspapers. All-in package holidays can be the least expensive way to go. Excel Airways (tel: 0870 320 7777, <www.xl.com>) offers some of the cheapest flights. British Airways (tel: 0870 850 9850, <www.britishairways.com>), and the national carrier Iberia (tel: 0870 609 0500, <www.iberia.com>) in the UK, also have promotional deals.

There are no direct flights to Tenerife from the US. Airlines go via major European airports, with the Spanish state airline Iberia (tel: 1-800 772-4642) going via Madrid, from where internal flights connect to all the Canary Islands. Flights can take 12–13 hours and cost around $1,000.

By ship: Trasmediterránea <www.trasmediterranea.es> has a limited number of sailings from Cádiz. For further details contact in the UK: Southern Ferries, 30 Churton Street, London, SW1V 2LP, tel: 0844 815 7785, <www.southernferries.co.uk>; in Spain: Compañía Trasmediterránea, Avenida de Europa, 10, 28108 Alcobendas, Madrid (tel: 902 45 46 45); on Tenerife: Compañía Trasmediterránea, Los Cristianos, fax only: 922 79 61 78.

GUIDES AND TOURS

The island is comprehensively covered by tour operators, whose coaches take tourists anywhere and everywhere that is worth seeing, both day and night. Check with the local tourist office, or at your hotel's reception desk.

H

HEALTH AND MEDICAL CARE

Non-EU visitors should have private medical insurance, and although there are reciprocal arrangements between EU countries, it is advisable for Britons to take out private insurance, too. The EHIC card, which entitles EU citizens to free health care, is available in the UK from post offices or online at <www.ehic.org.uk>. Before being treated it is advisable to check that the doctor is working within the Spanish Health Service.

Dental treatment is not generally available under this system, so private insurance is strongly advised.

Farmácias (chemists/drugstores) can deal with a number of health problems, and recommend remedies. They are usually open during normal shopping hours. After hours, at least one per town remains open all night. Called a *farmácia de guardia*, its location is posted in the window of all other *farmácias* nearby and printed in the local newspapers.

Where's the nearest (all-night) chemist?	¿Dónde está la farmácia (de guardia) más cercana?
I need a doctor/dentist.	Necesito un médico/dentista.
sunburn/sunstroke	quemadura del sol/una insolación
an upset stomach	molestias de estómago
Is this service public or private?	¿Es este servicio público o privado?

HOLIDAYS *(día de fiesta)*

In addition to these Spanish national holidays, many purely local and lesser religious, civic and other holidays are celebrated in various towns of the archipelago *(see page 95)*.

1 January	*Año Nuevo*	New Year's Day
6 January	*Epifanía*	Epiphany
1 May	*Día del Trabajo*	Labour Day
15 August	*Asunción/Nuestra Señora de la Candelaria*	Assumption
12 October	*Día de la Hispanidad*	Discovery of America Day (Columbus Day)
1 November	*Todos los Santos*	All Saints' Day
6 December	*Día de la Constitución*	Constitution Day
8 December	*Inmaculada Concepción*	Immaculate Conception
25 December	*Navidad*	Christmas Day

Movable dates:

Carnaval	Week of Shrove Tuesday
Jueves Santo	Maundy Thursday
Viernes Santo	Good Friday
Corpus Christi	Corpus Christi

L

LANGUAGE

The Spanish spoken in the Canary Islands is a little different from that of the mainland. For instance, islanders don't lisp when they pronounce the letters c or z. The language of the Canaries is spoken with a slight lilt, reminiscent of the Caribbean, and a number of New World words

Do you speak English?	**¡Habla usted inglés?**
I don't speak Spanish.	**No hablo español.**

and expressions are used. The most common are *guagua* (pronounced wah-wah), meaning bus, and *papa* (potato). In tourist areas German, English and some French is often spoken, or at least understood.

The *Berlitz Spanish Phrasebook and Dictionary* covers most situations you may encounter in your travels in Tenerife.

LOST PROPERTY *(Objetos perdidos)*

The first thing to do is to retrace your steps. If you still cannot find the missing item, report the loss to the Municipal Police or the Guardia Civil (see POLICE).

I've lost my wallet/ pocketbook/passport.	**He perdido mi cartera/bolso/ pasaporte.**

MAPS

Maps are generally available from hotel receptions and tourist offices, though walking maps are less easy to come by, and should be purchased if possible before going to the area in which you plan to walk.

MEDIA

Radio and television *(radio; televisión)*: Many hotels have satellite television with several stations in many languages. The larger ones all include some English-language news and tourist information in their programming. English-language radio stations on Tenerife include Radio FM 95.3 MHz, Power FM 91–2 MHz and Waves FM 96.8 MHz.

Newspapers and periodicals: Many major British and continental papers are on sale in the Canaries on the day of publication. There are a number of English-language publications with Canarian news and tourist information, which are not very evenly distributed. These include *Tenerife News*, a fortnightly paper, also available on the web

(<www.tenerifenews.com>), the monthly *Living Tenerife* <www.livingtenerife.com>, and the on-line *News Canarias* <www.ic-web.com>, as well as various property-based publications.

There is also a good annual restaurant guide, *¡Qué Bueno!* in English and Spanish.

MONEY MATTERS

Currency: The monetary unit in the Canary Islands, as throughout Spain, is the euro, symbolised €. Bank notes are available in denominations of 500, 200, 100, 50, 20, 10 and 5. The euro is sub-divided into 100 cents and there are coins available for €1 and €2 and for 50, 20, 10, 5, 2 and 1 cent.

Currency exchange. Banks are the best place to exchange currency. *Casas de cambio* stay open outside banking hours, as do some other businesses displaying a *cambio* sign. All larger hotels will also change guests' money, but the rate is slightly less favourable than at the bank. Both banks and exchange offices pay slightly less for cash than for travellers' cheques. Always take your passport when you go to change money.

Credit cards. Major cards are widely recognised on Tenerife, although smaller businesses still tend to prefer cash. Visa/Eurocard/MasterCard are the cards that are most generally accepted. Credit and debit cards are also useful for obtaining cash from ATMs – cash machines – which are to be found in all towns and resorts. They offer the most convenient way of obtaining cash and will usually give you the best exchange rate.

Travellers' cheques. Hotels, shops, restaurants and travel agencies all cash travellers' cheques, and so do banks, where you are likely to get a better rate (you will need to show your passport). It is safest to cash small amounts at any one time, thereby retaining some of your holiday funds in cheques, which you can keep in the hotel safe. Banking hours are usually from 9am–2pm Monday to Friday, and on public holidays (see HOLIDAYS).

Where's the nearest bank (currency exchange office)?	¿Dónde está el banco (la oficina de cambio) más cercana?
I want to change some dollars/pounds.	Quiero cambiar dólares/ libres esterlina.
Do you accept travellers' checks?	¿Acepta usted cheques de viajero?
Can I pay with this credit card?	¿Puedo pagar con esta tarjeta de crédito?

O

OPENING HOURS

Shops, offices and other businesses generally observe the afternoon siesta, opening from Monday to Saturday 9am–1pm and 4–8pm (some on Saturday morning only). In tourist areas many places don't open until 10am, but they then stay open all day. Post offices are open from 8.30am to 2.30pm.

Most shops and businesses are closed on Sunday even in the most commercialised resorts.

P

POLICE (policía)

There are three police forces in Tenerife, as in the rest of Spain. The *Guardia Civil* (Civil Guard) is the main force. Each town also has its own *Policía Municipal* (municipal police), whose uniform varies depending on the town and season but is mostly a combination of blue and grey. The third force, the *Cuerpo Nacional de Policía*, is a national anti-crime unit whose officers wear a light-brown uniform.

All police officers are armed. Spanish policing is strict but officers are generally courteous to foreign visitors.

| Where is the nearest police station? | ¿Dónde está la comisaría más cercana? |

POST OFFICES *(correos)*

Post offices are for mail and telegrams, not phone calls. Stamps *(sellos)* are sold at any tobacconist's *(estancos)* and by most shops selling postcards. See the website <www.correos.es>. Mailboxes are painted yellow. Slots marked *extranjero* are for letters abroad.

| Where is the (nearest) post office?
A stamp for this letter/postcard, please. | ¿Dónde está la oficina de correos (más cercana)?
Por favor, un sello para esta carta/tarjeta. |

PUBLIC TRANSPORT

Airlines: A number of airlines fly between the islands, and are not much more expensive than ferries. Binter Canarias (tel: 902 39 13 92, <www.binternet.com>), a subsidiary of Iberia, has the most flights. Spanair (tel: 902 13 14 15, <www.spanair.com>) also has flights.

Bus services: Buses *(guaguas)* are run by TITSA (Transporte Interurbanos de Tenerife SA, tel: 922 531 300, <www.titsa.com>) and are frequent, fast and cheap. They cover all major and most minor destinations on the island. Tickets can be bought on board, but if you buy a BONO-BUS card with either €12 or €30 credit on it from a newsagent beforehand, you will get half-price travel. Timetables can be obtained at bus depots, tourist offices or online.

Tram services: In 2007 a new tram service opened, connecting Santa Cruz and La Laguna. It is clean, efficient and speedy and a good way of avoiding traffic. Ticket prices start at €1.25 for a single journey. See <www.metrotenerife.com> for timetables.

Ferry services: Fred Olsen Lines runs speedy services to most of the other islands in the Canaries. Its jetfoil takes 1 hour to Agaete on Gran Canaria, where there is a free connecting bus to Las Palmas, taking another hour. Fred Olsen also serves the islands of La Gomera, La Palma and El Hierro from Los Cristianos. Further information from Fred Olsen SA, Dr Zerolo 14, Santa Cruz de Tenerife (tel: 902 10 01 07, <www.fredolsen.es>). Note that if you have bought your ticket in advance, it must be confirmed at the desk half an hour before departure. Naviera Armas (tel: 922 53 40 50, <www.naviera armas.com>) runs ferries from Los Cristianos to La Gomera, and from Santa Cruz to all of the other Canary Islands. Trasmediterránea (tel: 902 45 46 45, <www.trasmediterranea.es>) runs ferries to Gran Canaria, taking 4 hours for the 63-km (39-mile) crossing.

R

RELIGION

The predominant religion of Tenerife is Catholicism, which is deeply observed. The Madonna of Candelaria is the patron saint of the whole Canary Islands, bringing pilgrims from all of Spain. On Tenerife the bishop's see is in La Laguna. Tourists should respect local sensibilities and not enter churches dressed for the beach, or intrude on public and private prayer.

T

TAXES

Impuestos Generalisado Indirecto Canario (IGIC) is levied on all goods and services at a rate of 5 percent.

TAXIS

The letters SP *(servicio público)* on the front and rear bumpers of a car indicate that it is a taxi; it might also have a green light in the front

How much is it to Hotel Mencey/the town centre?	¿Cuanto es al Hotel Mencey/ al centro?

windscreen or a green sign indicating '*libre*' when it is free. Fixed prices are displayed on a board at the main taxi rank, giving the fares to the most popular destinations. These are reasonable, and in general taxis, which are easily found in urban areas, provide an inexpensive method of transport. If in doubt, just ask the driver before setting off.

TELEPHONES *(teléfono)*

Phone booths *(kioskos)* accept coins and cards *(tarjetas telefónicas)* available from tobacconists. Instructions in English, along with area codes for different countries, are displayed clearly. International calls are expensive, so be sure to have a plentiful supply of coins or enough money on your card. For international direct dialling, wait for the dial tone, then dial 00, wait for a second tone and dial the country code, area code (minus the initial zero) and number. In some places there are *cabinas*, phone cabins where you make your call and pay afterwards.

For American visitors, calling directly from your hotel room is expensive unless you are using a calling card, or some other similar system, from a long-distance supplier such as AT&T or MCI. Find out from the supplier which free connection number is applicable to Spain (they are different for each country) before you leave, as these numbers are not always easily available once there.

Check with your service provider before leaving home to see if your mobile phone will operate from the Canary Islands, and within Tenerife.

Operator: The number for the international operator is 025.

Country codes: For the US and Canada dial 1, Great Britain 44, Australia 61, New Zealand 64, the Republic of Ireland 353 and South Africa 27.

Local codes: The code for Spain is +34. For the Canary Islands a prefix must always be dialled, even for local calls: Province of Santa Cruz de Tenerife (Tenerife, El Hierro, La Gomera and La Palma) 922; Province of Las Palmas de Gran Canaria (Gran Canaria, Lanzarote and Fuerteventura) 928.

TIME DIFFERENCES

In winter the Canary Islands maintain Greenwich Mean Time, which is one hour behind most European countries, including Spain, but the same as the UK. For the rest of the year the islands go on summer time, as does Spain – keeping the one-hour difference.

Winter time chart:

Los Angeles 4am	New York 7am	London noon	**Canaries noon**	Madrid 1pm

TIPPING (propinas)

Since a service charge is often included in restaurant bills, tipping is not obligatory. Ten percent of the bill is usual for taxi drivers, bar staff, waiters and hairdressers. Also tip porters and maids a few euros, depending on length of stay.

TOILETS

The most commonly used expressions for toilets in the Canaries are *servicios* or *aseos*, though you may also hear or see WC ('dooblavay say') and *retretes*. Public conveniences are well maintained and located alongside most beaches. Hotels, bars and restaurants usually have lavatories and it is considered polite to buy a coffee if you do drop into a bar to use their facilities.

Where are the lavatories?	**¿Dónde están los servicios?**

TOURIST INFORMATION

Information on the Canary Islands may be obtained from <www.spain.info> or from **Spanish National Tourist Offices**, which include the following:

Canada: 2 Bloor Street West, 34th Floor, Toronto, Ontario M4W 3E2, tel: (416) 961-3131, fax: (416) 961-1992, email: <toronto@tourspain.es>.

UK: 79 New Cavendish Street, London, W1W 6XB, tel: 020 7317 2010 (visits by appointment), email: <londres@tourspain.es>, brochure line, tel: 08459 400180 (Republic of Ireland 0818 220 290).

US: Chicago: Water Tower Place, Suite 915 East, 845 North Michigan Avenue, Chicago, IL 60611, tel: (312) 642-1992, fax: (312) 642-9817, email: <chicago@tourspain.es>.

Los Angeles: 8383 Wilshire Boulevard, Suite 960, Beverly Hills, Los Angeles, CA 90211, tel: (323) 658 7195, fax: (323) 658-1061, email: <losangeles@tourspain.es>.

New York: 666 Fifth Avenue, 35th Floor, New York, NY 10103, tel: (212) 265-8822, fax: (212) 265-8864, email: <nuevayork@tourspain.es>.

Miami: 1395 Brickell Avenue, Miami, Florida, FL 33131, tel: (305) 358-1992, fax: (305) 358-8223, email: <miami@tourspain.es>.

In **Tenerife**, the main office for the whole island is the Cabildo Insular in Plaza de España, Santa Cruz de Tenerife, tel: 922 23 95 92, fax: 922 23 98 12, open Mon–Fri 9am–6pm, Sat 9am–1pm. The Tenerife tourist board has three websites: <www.webtenerife.com>, <www.tenerife.es> and <www.puntoinfo.idecnet.com>.

Information may also be obtained from the following **local tourist information offices**:

Adeje: Avenida Rafael Puig 1 (by the Playa de Troya), tel: 922 75 06 33; open Mon–Fri 10am–5pm; July–Sept Mon–Fri 10am–4pm.

Aeropuerto Tenerife-Sur Reina Sofía (Arrivals Terminal): tel: 922 39 20 37; open Mon–Fri 9am–9pm, Sat–Sun 9am–5pm; July–Sept Mon–Fri 9am–7pm, Sat–Sun 9am–5pm.

Candelaria/Las Caletillas: Plaza del CIT, tel: 922 50 04 15; open Mon–Fri 8am–8pm, Sat 8am–1pm.

El Médano: Plaza de los Principes de España, tel: 922 17 60 02; open Mon–Fri 9am–3pm, Sat 9am–1pm; July–Sept Mon–Fri 9am–2pm, Sat 9am–noon.

La Laguna: La Carrera 7, Bajo, Casa de Alvaredo Bracamonte, tel: 922 63 11 94; open daily 9am–5pm.

La Orotava: Calle Calvario 4, tel: 922 32 30 41; open Mon–Fri 8.30am–6pm.

Las Galletas: Dionisio González Delgado Promenade, tel: 922 73 01 33; open Mon–Fri 9am–3.30pm, Sat 9am–1pm.

Los Cristianos: Centro Cultural (Casa de La Cultura, opposite the Mobil fuel station), Plaza de Pescador, tel: 922 75 71 37; open Mon–Fri 9am–3.30pm, Sat 9am–1pm.

Playa de las Américas, Arona: Avenida Rafael Puig 19, tel: 922 79 76 68; open Mon–Fri 9am–9pm, Sat 9am–3.30pm.

Playa de las Vistas: Paseo de las Vistas s/n, tel: 922 78 70 11; open Mon–Fri 9am–9pm, Sat 9am–3.30pm.

Puerto de la Cruz: Casa de la Aduana, Calle Las Lonjas, tel: 922 38 60 00; open daily 9am–8pm.

Santa Cruz de Tenerife: Cabildo Insular (Plaza de Espana), tel: 922 23 95 92; open Mon–Fri 9am–6pm, Sat 9am–1pm; July–Sept Mon–Fri 8am–5pm, Sat 9am–noon.

Santiago del Teide: Centro Comercial Seguro de Sol, Local 35, Manuel Ravelo 20, tel: 922 86 03 48; open Mon–Fri 8am–2.30pm.

TRAVELLERS WITH DISABILITIES

Tenerife's climate makes it favourite place for recuperation, and it is well adapted to the needs of travellers with disabilities. There are wheelchair ramps at the major airports and many larger apartments and hotels make provision for disabled guests. Some of the more modern resorts also provide ramps to cross pavements. The facilities at Los Cristianos are renowned among disabled travellers and the Marisol Resort in particular specialises in holidays for such guests and their families. Access Travel in the United Kingdom (tel: 01942 888 844) is one operator that goes there.

Wheelchairs can be hired from Ortopedia Hospitalaria Lero, Puerto De La Cruz (tel: 922 75 02 89, fax: 922 75 02 83) or Orange Badge, Local No. 9 Cristian Sur, Avenida Amsterdam, Los Cristianos (tel/fax: 922 79 73 55, <www.orangebadge.com>).

W

WATER *(agua)*

Tap water is safe to drink but can have a tang to it, so people generally prefer to drink bottled water: *con gas* (sparkling) and *sin gas* (still). Remember that water is scarce, so don't waste it.

WEBSITES

There are Internet cafés in Santa Cruz, Puerto de la Cruz, Los Cristianos and Playa de las Américas. Libraries have Internet facilities, but you cannot use them for emails.

There a number of websites with useful up-to-date information about Tenerife. The following is just a selection:

www.spain.info Spanish tourist office website
www.turismodecanarias.com Canary Islands tourism website
www.webtenerife.com Tenerife tourist office site
www.tenerife.es Tenerife tourist office site
www.puntoinfo.idecnet.com Tenerife tourist office site
www.tenerifenews.com local fortnightly paper on-line
www.thinkspain.com Spanish regional news
www.ecoturismocanarias.com rural tourism accommodation

Puerto Azul € *Lomo 24, tel/fax: 922 38 32 13, <www.puerto-azul. com>*. A pleasant, small, modern, two-star hotel just off the central Plaza del Charco. Eight of the 26 basic rooms are singles and two have large terraces. The roof terrace is open to all guests.

San Telmo €€ *Calle San Telmo 18, tel: 922 38 58 53, fax: 922 38 59 91*. Right on the seafront, with balconied rooms overlooking the sea, which splashes against the rocks all night long. Not posh, this is a delightful, old-fashioned hotel, with a breezy seaside feel. Buffet breakfast is included in the price and there's a small rooftop pool.

THE NORTHWEST

GARACHICO

Hotel Rural El Patio €€€ *Finca Malpaís, El Guincho, tel: 922 13 32 80, fax: 922 83 00 89, <www.hotelpatio.com>*. Inland and just east of Garachico, the hotel is on a banana plantation in a house that is said to date from the 16th century. There are 26 bedrooms decorated in rural style. Walks head off through the gardens and plantations and there is a heated pool and restaurant.

Hotel San Roque €€€€ *Calle Esteban de Ponte 32, tel: 922 13 34 35, fax: 922 13 34 06, <www.hotelsanroque.com>*. This 18th-century mansion in the centre of town has a warm, stylish interior. Rooms are individually furnished and decorated with works by contemporary local artists. There is a swimming pool and rooftop solarium.

Pensión El Jardín € *Esteban de Ponte 8, tel: 922 83 02 45*. This family-run *pensión* is in an old townhouse with patio. The bedrooms leading off the first-floor landing have no windows, but are spacious and comfortable with original furniture. The large family attic room has rooftop views. The hotel can also organise diving trips.

La Quinta Roja €€€ *Glorieta de San Francisco s/n, tel: 922 13 33 77, fax: 922 13 33 60, <www.quintaroja.com>*. This lovely mansion in the quiet central square is a survivor of the 18th-century earthquake. It was home of the Marqués of Quinta Roja and is typical of island baroque style. Opened in 2002, it is very much plugged into local activities, organising excursions into the countryside. Don't miss the turtles in the outside pool.

THE SOUTH

EL MÉDANO

Hotel Médano €€–€€€ *Paseo Picacho 4, tel: 922 17 70 00, fax: 922 17 60 48, <www.hotelmedano.com>.* On the beach with four sun terraces, overlooking the sea and the Montaña Roja. Offers windsurfing, kitesurfing, scuba diving, trekking, cycling and golf.

Playa Sur Tenerife €€€ *E-38612 El Medano, tel: 922 17 61 20, fax: 922 17 63 37, <www.hotelplayasurtenerife.com>.* Isolated in the middle of a long stretch of beach, this has long been a windsurfers' choice, with boards for hire. It faces the beach on either side, so all rooms have balconies with views. There is a pool and bar.

GRANADILLA DE ABONA

Hotel Rural Senderos de Abona €€€ *Calle la Iglesia 5, tel: 922 77 02 00, fax: 922 77 03 08, <www.senderosdeabona.com>.* An enclosed hotel that was once the post office, in the quiet streets of Granadilla. The rooms are in period and there is a good restaurant as well as a collection of tools and implements in a 'museum'. Only the clock on the church opposite disturbs the peace, every quarter of an hour.

GÜÍMAR

Casona Santo Domingo €€ *Calle Santo Domingo 32, tel/fax: 922 51 02 29, <www.casonasantodomingo.com>.* An elegant, central *hotel rural* dating from the 16th century, with pitch pine balconies, period furniture and a common sitting room with coffee-table books about the area. The restaurant serves a menu of local dishes.

Hotel Rural Finca Salamanca €€€ *Carretera Güimar–El Puertito, Km1.5, tel: 922 51 45 30, fax: 922 51 40 61, <www.hotel-*

fincasalamanca.com>. A manor house, in a country estate, that has been converted into a charming small hotel for those who want peace and quiet and still enjoy top class facilities. 16 rooms.

ADEJE

La Fonda Central €€ *Calle Grande 26, tel: 922 781 550*. An attractive noble house, with courtyard, dating from the 18th century, situated in the old part of town; the hotel has 11 rooms en suite, a solarium, bar and restaurant.

LOS CRISTIANOS

Arona Gran Hotel €€€€ *Avenida Juan Carlos I 38, tel: 922 75 06 78, fax: 922 75 02 43, <www.aronahotel.com>*. On a slightly scrubby stretch of beach at the end of Los Cristianos harbour, all rooms are modern and have a terrace overlooking the water. Sports facilities, restaurants and bars, and a wonderful atrium lobby bedecked with green plants hanging from each floor. 400 rooms.

Hotel Andrea's €€ *Avenida del Valle Menendez, tel: 922 79 00 12, fax: 922 79 42 70, <www.hotelesreveron.com>*. One of the few non four-star hotels in Los Cristianos, this is a modern block that's easy to find as you come into town. Try to get a room overlooking the street as inner rooms are a bit gloomy. No breakfast, but connected to a downstairs pizza restaurant. Clean, friendly and good value.

La Paloma € *Peatonal Berlin 7, tel: 922 79 01 98*. One of half a dozen *pensiónes* around the old part of town. The full-blown restaurant downstairs is one of the better pavement places to eat in town.

PLAYA DE LAS AMÉRICAS

Flamingo Suites €€€€ *Avenida España s/n, Playa de las Américas, tel: 922 71 84 00, fax: 922 71 84 01*. These luxury apartments in the heart of Playa de las Américas are considered Tenerife's most exclusive private club. They have every modern facility, including Jacuzzi tubs, plunge pools and daily maid service. 18 suites.

Gran Tacande €€€ *Calle Walter Paetzman s/n, tel: 922 74 64 00, fax: 922 74 63 77, <www.gran-tacande-hotel.com>*. One of the Dreamplace resorts that tries to look like a swanky village, built in various Canarian architectural styles. By the sea with heated salt-water pool. There are 207 rooms, plus the Royal or Imperial suites with their own Jacuzzi, reception and lounges.

Mare Nostrum Resort €€€€ *Avenda de las Américas s/n, tel: 922 75 75 45, fax: 922 75 32 26, <www.expogrupo.com>*. Fantasy clas-sical land in one of five 5-star hotels – Sir Anthony, Cleopatra, Julio Cesar, Marco Antonio and Mediterranean Palace (with rooftop nud-ist zone and pool). Together they provide more than a thousand rooms, 102 with their own private pools, with thalassotherapy a spe-ciality, and 13 restaurants. You won't even know you are in Tenerife.

VILAFLOR

El Hotel Nogal €€€ *Camino Real s/n La Escalona, tel: 922 72 60 50, fax: 922 72 58 53, <www.hotelnogal.com>*. Half way to heaven, this secluded 19th-century estate between Arona and Vilaflor has been converted into a hotel by its owners, descendants of the orginal Linares family. There are 40 double rooms tastefully furnished.

Hotel El Sombrerito €–€€ *Calle Santa Catalina 15, tel: 922 70 90 52, fax: 922 70 93 52, <www.hotelelsombrerito.es>*. Enjoy tra-ditional Canarian hospitality at this family-run *pensión*. The restored inn is decorated with rural artefacts and the hotel's restau-rant serves local cuisine. You can even feed their goats. 21 rooms.

Hotel VillAlba €€ *Carretera San Roque s/n, tel: 922 70 99 30, fax: 922 70 93 41, <www.hotelvillalba.com>*. 'The highest hotel in Spain' is the boast of this modern hotel 1,660m (5,450ft) above sea level. There are 22 spacious rooms with all facilities including DVDs, gym and Jacuzzi. All kinds of activities in the area are available through the hotel, including hang-gliding, mountain biking and climbing.

Recommended Restaurants

Listed below is a pot pouri of restaurants to be found around the island. They have been chosen because of their originality, setting, convenience or simply for the quality of their food. *Tinerfeños* eat late by northern European standards, starting lunch around 2 or 3pm, and dinner around 9 or 10pm.

Eating is not expensive on the island. Fixed-price menus *(menú del día)*, generally available at lunchtime only, can be as little as €7 for three courses and a glass of wine. To give you an idea of price (for two; a three-course meal including a bottle of house wine), we have used the following symbols:

€€€€   over 120 euros
€€€   50–80 euros
€€   20–50 euros
€   under 20 euros

THE NORTHEAST

ANAGA

Cruz dei Carmen € *Las Mercedes Km6, tel: 922 25 00 62*. An ideal stop, by the Cruz del Carmen *mirador*, when exploring the Anaga Hills. Good solid Canarian cooking, with both meat and fish soups and home-made sweets, in three spacious dining rooms.

LA LAGUNA

Casa Maquila €€ *Callejón de Maquila s/n, tel: 922 25 70 20*. This is a reliable local, with several individual rooms and regulars who chat at the bar. Parrot fish and squid are on the menu, together with chickpea staples, and simple dishes of mushrooms, peas and ham. Look out for the Tacoronte on the wine list.

Las Cazuelitas del Marqués €€€ *Calle Herradores 105, tel: 922 25 19 75*. An intimate, friendly establishment with a busy domestic interior. Locals pop in for a drink and chat with the chef-owner, Adolfo González and his wife, Aida. Portions are generous and the menu is innovative.

La Posada de los Mosqueteros €€ *Calle Santo Domingo 24, tel: 922 25 49 65.* A *tasca* known for its selection of hams and cheeses, and local dishes such as pheasant and rabbit with prawns. Closed Sundays.

LOS NARANJEROS

Restaurant La Vara €€ *Carretera General del Norte Km398, tel: 922 56 38 20/56 14 11.* Set in an old house, with a number of dining rooms, this is one of many popular restaurants between La Laguna and Tacoronte that fill up with diners at weekend lunchtimes. The house specialities include soups made with local wines. Other soups are conjured up from boiled salted fish. Roast meats are also in plentiful supply.

SANTA CRUZ

El Aguila €€ *Plaza Alféreces Provisionales, tel: 922 27 31 56.* This restaurant is set in a central pedestrian square with plenty to watch – including a large screen outside when a big football game is on. Has an extensive selection of *tapas* with large *parillas* of fish or meat – go to the counter and point to the ones that take your fancy.

Bodega San Sebastián €€ *Avenida San Sebastián 55, tel: 922 21 68 53.* This is one of the oldest *bodegas* in the town. You can choose from the scores of different wines they have to offer.

El Coto del Antonio €€ *Calle General Goded 13, tel: 922 27 21 05.* An intimate, *tasca*-like restaurant off the Rambla, serving Canarian and Basque food. The menu includes such dishes as baby bean salad with lobster, and goat in almond sauce.

Los Cuatro Postes €€ *Calle Emilio Calzadilla 5, tel: 922 28 73 94, fax: 922 24 25 39.* Tucked up a side street near the Plaza de España this excellent restaurant is a favourite of those in the know.

Great Spanish food served in a friendly, atmospheric dining room. Popular with families at weekend lunchtimes.

La Hierbita € *Calle Clavel 19, tel: 922 24 46 17, <www.lahierbita. com>.* An old house with many small, well-decorated rooms on two floors. Rabbit stew and other good local dishes. Try the *hierbita* liqueur made by the owner.

THE NORTH

EL SAUZAL

Casa del Vino La Baranda €€€ *Autopista General del Norte Km21, tel: 922 57 25 35, <www.cabtfe.es/casa-vino>.* The restaurant in this elegant 17th-century estate, now occupied by the wine museum, serves good modern Canarian food, and is the best place to try – and seek advice about – Canarian wines. There is also a *tasca* bar that has views from the terrace down to the sea. Closed on Mondays.

ICOD DE LOS VINOS

La Cueva de San Marcos €€ *Carretera del Amparo 97, tel: 922 81 24 42.* This *finca* located right in the middle of the wine-growing area makes and bottles 20,000 litres of its own red and white wine every year. The informal restaurant, with four terrace tables, offers excellent Canarian home-cooking.

LA OROTAVA

El Engazo €€ *Finca Tafuriaste, Las Candias 17, tel: 922 33 35 56.* The *finca* of the Pontes Mendéz estate was bought by the current chef Manuel Luis Dominguez in 1963, since when it has acquired a reputation for friendliness and good local dishes, such as spare ribs with corn on the cob. Closed Thursdays and Sunday evenings.

Kiú €€ *Casa Lercaro, Calle Colegio 7, tel: 922 32 37 38, <www. casalercaro.es>.* This restaurant is housed in a beautifully restored traditional mansion at the heart of La Orotava's old town. There is an outside seating area so that diners can enjoy the view. The menu is highly original, including starters such as local sausage with fried lettuce leaves.

Sabor Canario €€ *Calle Carrera 17, tel: 922 32 27 93.* When visiting La Orotava's historic centre, you need to eat in an old townhouse such as this, which dates from 1580. The dishes are traditional too, including rabbit in *solmerejo* sauce, and various manifestations of *gofio* (roasted barley flour). It also has a good selection of wines.

PUERTO DE LA CRUZ

Casa de Miranda €€ *Calle Santo Domingo 13 (Plaza de Europa), tel: 922 37 38 71.* This attractive Canarian mansion, with wooden beams, floors and staircases, dates from 1730. The *bodeguita* on the lower floor has a selection of hams and cheeses. The restaurant upstairs specialises in fish and shellfish dishes, as well as serving wines produced on the premises.

La Gañaninía €€€ *Camino El Durazno s/n, tel: 922 37 10 00.* Located up towards the motorway near the Abaco museum-house, this is the converted stable of an 18th-century farmhouse, which has wonderful views over Puerto de la Cruz. The menu is Canarian, with *tapas* dishes.

The Oriental €€€ *Avenida Richard J. Yeoward, tel: 922 38 14 00.* Located within the Hotel Botánico, the speciality is Thai cookery with Pan-Asiatic touches. The ambiance here is formal and the cuisine is enticing. Open for dinner every evening.

El Peñon €€ *Calle José María del Campo, tel: 922 37 15 76.* Forced to move out of their old fisherman's quarters, the owners of the Bodegón Casa Antigua have renamed their restaurant and moved to a less salubrious location, beneath an apartment block opposite the football stadium. Fortunately, the high standard of grilled meats and fish remains and the atmosphere is lively and local.

Régulo €€€ *Calle Pérez Zamora 16, tel: 922 38 45 06*. One of the best restaurants in Puerto de la Cruz, Régulo occupies a typical Canarian 18th-century house with balconies around a delightful patio. Specialities of the house include *lapas a la plancha* (grilled limpet shells) and *solomillo relleno de camembert* (fillet steak with camembert stuffing). Open for lunch and dinner, closed Sundays and all July.

La Rosa di Bari €€ *Calle El Lomo 23, tel: 922 36 85 23*. This popular Italian restaurant is set in a small, tastefully decorated house in La Ranilla, Puerto de La Cruz's fisherman's quarter. Dishes on offer include a number of unique reworkings of traditional Italian favourites. The fresh pastas and seafood dishes are particularly good. Closed September.

La Tasquita de Min €€ *Calle Mequinez, tel: 922 37 18 34*. A reliable and hugely popular spot for excellent *tapas* and local dishes. Ask for the specials. Good, speedy service. Closed Mondays.

TEGUESTE

Casa Tomás € *Camino del Portezuelo 2, tel: 922 63 69 71*. Homemade Canarian food, dishes including spare ribs with potatoes and chickpea stews. Busy at weekends.

El Drago €€€ *Calle Marqués de Celada 2, tel: 922 54 30 01, <www.mesoneldrago.com>*. A restaurant worth looking out for, El Drago is an award-winning establishment run by Carlos Gamonal Jiménez and his sons. They serve some of the best Canarian dishes on the island, much of it their own creation, such as watercress soup with yam, red onion, cheese and *gofio*.

THE NORTHWEST

BUENAVISTA DEL NORTE

Rincón del Norte €€ *Avenida Juan Méndez el Viejo 10, tel: 922 12 73 01*. This restaurant serves up both international and local dishes, with daily variations, including *tapas*. The owner, José Méndez Baez, speaks English. Closed Wednesdays.

GARACHICO

Hotel San Roque €€€€ *Calle Esteban de Ponte 32, tel: 922 13 34 35.* Eat in a small dining room or at tables around the pool. The cuisine is as eclectic as the ambiance. Expect to find such delicacies as *daurade au sel* (fish baked in rock salt) and *paella duo* (made with vegetables and squid).

Isla Baja €€ *Esteban de Ponte 5.* An old town house with a cool courtyard and a model of the volcanic eruption that destroyed the town. Traditional local dishes.

MASCA

Chez Arlette € *tel: 922 86 34 59.* A delightful setting, looking down over the Barranco, and with a shady garden with hammocks and palms. Serves good local food including cactus juice and fresh goat's cheese. Closed Saturday.

THE SOUTH

CHAYOFA

La Finca del Arte €€ *Calle Centro 1, tel: 922 72 91 03, <www. fincadelarte.com>.* Situated between Playa de las Américas and Arona, this former tomato packing factory is run by Wolfgang Eggar, and it functions as an art gallery for local talent as well as a café and bistro. Good to drop in to any time of day; it livens up on Sundays with a jazz brunch.

GUÍA DE ISORA

Casa Juana €€€ *Calle Virgen de la Candelaria 12, tel: 922 86 61 26.* Famous for the home-cooking of its owner, Juana de Dios Navarro, this restaurant has a wood-fired oven to grill fresh fish.

LA CALETA

Masía del Mar €€ *Calle El Muella 3, tel: 922 71 08 95*. This great harbourside fish restaurant offers a real flavour of the Tenerife coast. Set in a restored warehouse dating from 1568, it serves some of the freshest fish and the most authentic dishes available on the coast.

LOS ABRIGOS

Restaurante Los Abrigos €€ *Paseo Maritimo, tel: 922 17 02 64, <www.pescan.net/rteabrigos>*. Wonderful port-side restaurant with extensive menu of fish, from *abadejo* (pollack) to *vieja* (parrot fish). Crowded at weekend lunchtimes. Closed on Wednesdays, but the next door Perlas de Mar (closed Mondays) has a similarly serious fish menu.

El Tizón €€€ *Calle La Marina 13, tel: 922 17 03 26*. A pleasantly decorated upmarket restaurant with a variety of dishes, especially from the sea, including anchovies with peppers and salmon with pasta. It has an extensive wine list, and prides itself on good coffee.

LOS CRISTIANOS

La Paloma €€, *La Paloma 4, tel: 922 79 22 49*. One of the better places to eat Spanish food in Los Cristianos; serves *tapas* and other local dishes. For more authentic fare, try some of the *tascas* on Calle Noruega, such as El Faro.

Rose's Cantina €€ *Urb. Oasis del Sur, tel: 922 75 19 72*. Tourists enjoy this cheerful touch of Mexico on the island, with staff suitably dressed and refreshing margaritas available at the bar. *Enchiladas* and *fajitas* are always on the menu that includes Speedy Gonzalez prawns.

El Sol €€ *Peatonal Roma, s/n, Los Cristianos, tel: 922 79 05 69*. Classic French cuisine is the speciality of the house in this highly recommended restaurant. Open for dinner only, closed Monday.

PLAYA DE LAS AMÉRICAS

Molino Blanco €€€€ *Avenida Austria 5, tel: 922 79 62 82, <www. molino-blanco.com>.* Charcoal grills and wood-fired ovens are the keynote of this well-known restaurant, which has such delights as suckling pig *(cochinillo)*, ostrich *(avastruz)*, hare *(ciervo)* and boar *(jabalí)* as well as fresh fish. It has an animated atmosphere in its three dining rooms, with live music, and the landmark white wind-mill makes it easy to find.

La Rana €€€ *Parque Santiago 4, tel: 922 75 25 22.* There's a touch of Gallego cooking in this attractive rural-style restaurant set amid the modern buildings. You can dine indoors or on the terrace, and a barbecue serves up lamb and veal chops. There is lots to choose from on the menu, and many Spanish come here to try it out.

Restaurante Poseidón €€€€ *Calle Londres 15, Playas del Duque, tel: 922 71 33 35.* The haute-cuisine restaurant of the Grand Hotel Anthelia Park. Beautifully presented, interesting dishes such as smoked salmon with hand-made goat's cheese, and tender fillets of sole stuffed with extremely tasty small shrimps and spinach.

Restaurante Gran Reserva €€ *Calle Londres 4, tel: 922 71 44 92.* This low-key restaurant, just up from Playa Fañabe, has outdoor seating and serves great steaks.

Restaurante La Tasca €€€ *Gran Hotel Bahia del Duque, Gran Meliá, Avenida Bruselas s/n, tel: 922 74 69 00.* A Spanish restaurant in décor, style and cuisine, with staff in traditional costume. Familiar and unusual dishes feature on the menu.

SAN ISIDRO

Bodega El Jable €€ *Calle Betenjuí 9, tel: 922 39 06 98.* Twice winner of the Best Canarian Cuisine award, this is where to find creative local dishes. Try the watercress soup or the tuna *(albacora)* with dry fruit vinaigrette.